Activists, Rebels, and Reformers

Activists, Rebels, and Reformers

Volume 3: N-Z

PHILLIS ENGELBERT

Diane Sawinski, Editor

AN IMPRINT OF THE GALE GROUP

DETROIT · NEW YORK · SAN FRANCISCO
LONDON · BOSTON · WOODBRIDGE, CT

Activists, Rebels, and Reformers

Phillis Engelbert

Staff

Diane Sawinski, *U•X•L Senior Editor*
Stacy McConnell and Gerda-Ann Raffaelle, *U•X•L Editors*
Carol DeKane Nagel, *U•X•L Managing Editor*
Thomas L. Romig, *U•X•L Publisher*

Sarah Tomasek, *Permissions Specialist*
Renee McPhail, *Research Assistant to Author*

Dean Dauphinais, *Senior Editor, Imaging and Multimedia Content*
Pamela A. Reed, *Imaging Coordinator*
Robert Duncan, *Imaging Specialist*
Randy Bassett, *Imaging Supervisor*
Barbara J. Yarrow, *Manager, Imaging and Multimedia Content*

Pamela A. E. Galbreath, *Senior Art Director*
Kenn Zorn, *Product Design Manager*

Rita Wimberley, *Senior Buyer*
Dorothy Maki, *Manufacturing Manager*
Evi Seoud, *Assistant Manager, Composition Purchasing and Electronic Prepress*
Mary Beth Trimper, *Manager, Composition and Electronic Prepress*

Linda Mahoney, LM Design, *Typesetting*

Cover photograph of Rigoberta Menchú (with megaphone) reproduced by permission of AP/Wide World Photos. Cover photographs of Mary Harris "Mother" Jones and Frederick Douglass reproduced by permission of the Library of Congress.

Library of Congress Cataloging-in-Publication Data

Engelbert, Phillis.

Activists, rebels, & reformers / Phillis Engelbert ; Diane Sawinski, editor.

p. cm.

Includes bibliographical references and index.

ISBN 0-7876-4847-7 (set) — ISBN 0-7876-4848-5 (vol. 1) - ISBN 0-7876-4849-3 (vol. 2) —ISBN 0-7876-4850-7 (vol. 3)

1. Social reformers—Biography—Juvenile literature. 2. Political activists—Biography—Juvenile literature. 3. Dissenters—Biography—Juvenile literature. [1. Reformers. 2. Political activists. 3. Dissenters.] I. Title: Activists, rebels, and reformers. II. Sawinski, Diane M. III. Title.

HN17.5 .E534 2000
303.48'4'0922—dc21
[B]   00-34365

Printed in the United States of America

10 9 8 7 6 5 4 3 2 1

Contents

Volume 2: G–M

Volume 3: N–Z

Activists by Cause

Italic numerals indicate volume numbers.

Workers' rights

Reader's Guide

Activists, Rebels, and Reformers contains biographical sketches of sixty-eight individuals plus seven organizations that have helped shape the course of history. Prominent movers and shakers are covered, as well as lesser-known agitators, from a variety of times and places.

Activists and organizations featured include: Jane Addams, who fought for peace and the rights of women and poor immigrant workers in Chicago at the turn of the twentieth century; Amnesty International, an organization dedicated to upholding human rights around the world and freeing all "prisoners of conscience"; Mohandas Gandhi, who united the citizens of India to peacefully overthrow British rule in the 1940s; and Nelson Mandela, who guided South Africa through a relatively peaceful transition to a multiracial democracy in the 1990s after having spent twenty-five years as a political prisoner. The essays are intended to inform and inspire students, as well as to empower them with the knowledge that ordinary people can make a difference in community and world affairs.

Format

Activists, Rebels, and Reformers is arranged in alphabetical order over three volumes. Each biography is five to ten pages long. Sidebars containing short biographies of associated individuals, descriptions of writings by or about the person or organization in the entry, and other relevant and interesting information highlight the text. More than 120 photographs and illustrations help bring the subject matter to life. Difficult words are defined, cross-references to related entries are made within the text, and a further readings section accompanies each entry. Each volume concludes with a cumulative subject index, providing easy access to the people and movements discussed throughout *Activists, Rebels, and Reformers*.

Special thanks

The author offers most special thanks to Renee McPhail—research czarina, manuscript reader, and extraordinarily good friend. Appreciation is also due to U•X•L editors Diane Sawinski and Gerda-Ann Raffaelle for coordinating the final stages of this project; to University of Michigan Spanish professor Eliana Moya-Raggio and economist Dean Baker of the Washington, D.C.-based Center for Economic and Policy Research for their assistance with select entries; and to the following scholars and activists who suggested entries for inclusion: Rev. Joseph Summers, Ted Sylvester, Ingrid Kock, Kidada Williams, Susan Tachna, and Matt Calvert. Finally, sincere thanks go to Bill Shea and Ryan Patrick Shea—the best husband and son an author could hope for.

Comments and suggestions

We welcome your comments on *Activists, Rebels, and Reformers* as well as your suggestions for entries to be included in future volumes. Please write: Editors, *Activists, Rebels, and Reformers* U•X•L, 27500 Drake Rd., Farmington Hills, MI 48331–3535; call toll-free 1–800–877–4253; fax to 248–699–8097; or send e-mail via http://www.galegroup.com.

Advisory Board

Special thanks are due for the invaluable comments and suggestions provided by U•X•L's *Activists, Rebels, and Reformers* advisors:

- Tracey Easthope, Director of Environmental Health Project, Ecology Center, Ann Arbor, Michigan

- Frances Hasso, Assistant Professor of Sociology and Women's Studies, Oberlin College, Oberlin, Ohio

- Elizabeth James, Librarian, Center for Afroamerican and African Studies, University of Michigan, Ann Arbor, Michigan

- Premilla Nadasen, Assistant Professor of African-American History, Queens College, New York, New York

- Jan Toth-Chernin, Media Specialist, Greenhills School, Ann Arbor, Michigan

Timeline of Events

1818 English Quaker prison reformer **Elizabeth Fry** founds the British Ladies' Society for Promoting the Reformation of Female Prisoners.

1837 Abolitionists **Sarah and Angelina Grimké** undertake a speaking tour of New York State on behalf of the American Anti-Slavery Society.

1837 Attorney and politician **Horace Mann** successfully campaigns to establish a Massachusetts State Board of Education and becomes the board's first secretary. In that position he reforms the state's public school system, making it a model for the rest of the nation.

1847 **Frederick Douglass** begins publishing the antislavery paper *North Star* in Rochester, New York.

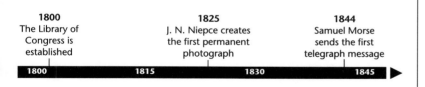

1800
The Library of
Congress is
established

1825
J. N. Niepce creates
the first permanent
photograph

1844
Samuel Morse
sends the first
telegraph message

1800	1815	1830	1845

1848 **Karl Marx** and Friedrich Engels publish *The Communist Manifesto,* calling on working people to overthrow their governments and establish a communist society.

1848 Women's rights convention is held at Seneca Falls, New York, to discuss women's suffrage and the abolition of slavery.

1850 **Harriet Tubman** makes her first of many journeys into the South to help slaves escape to freedom.

1850 Congress enacts the Fugitive Slave Act, which requires federal marshals to arrest any black person accused of being a runaway slave. This legislation results in the return to the South, and slavery, of many escaped slaves and free blacks in the North and intensifies the battle over slavery.

October 16, 1859 **John Brown** leads a group of twenty-one men on a failed raid of Harpers Ferry armory in Virginia in an attempt to spark an armed rebellion of slaves against their masters.

1865 Slavery is abolished with the passage of the Thirteenth Amendment.

1869 Suffragists **Elizabeth Cady Stanton** and Susan B. Anthony found the National Woman Suffrage Association (NWSA) to press for a constitutional amendment guaranteeing women the right to vote.

1886 Striking workers at Chicago's McCormick Harvesting Machine Company hold a rally in Haymarket Square. Seven police officers are killed by a dynamite bomb detonated at the rally, a crime for which eight union leaders are later convicted despite a lack of evidence. Four of those convicted are eventually hanged.

1850
The Compromise of 1850 is passed by Congress

1853
Potato chips are invented

1861–65
U.S. Civil War

1874
Dominion of Canada is created

1850 1860 1870 1880

1889 Social reformers **Jane Addams** and Ellen G. Starr inaugurate the community center and welfare agency called Hull House in Chicago.

1890 U.S. forces massacre between 150 and 370 Native Americans at Wounded Knee in South Dakota.

1890 The National American Woman Suffrage Association (NAWSA) is formed by the merger of two rival suffrage organizations: the National Woman Suffrage Association and the American Woman Suffrage Association.

1903 Labor leader **Mary Harris "Mother" Jones** leads thousands of youthful textile workers on a 125–mile march from Philadelphia to the New York home of President Theodore Roosevelt to protest child labor.

1911 Mexican revolutionary **Emiliano Zapata** issues his revolutionary manifesto, the *Plan de Alaya,* which advocates the overthrow of the government, the forcible repossession of lands stolen from farmers, and the redistribution of one-third of all plantation lands to peasants.

1912 Workplace safety advocate **Florence Kelley** successfully lobbies for the formation of the United States Children's Bureau, the nation's first child welfare agency.

1913 Feminists **Alice Paul** and Lucy Burns found the radical suffrage organization Congressional Union, which in 1917 becomes part of the National Woman's Party.

1915 Legendary labor leader **Joe Hill** is executed by firing squad in Utah for the alleged murders of a grocery store owner and his son.

1917 **American Friends Service Committee** is founded in Philadelphia to help conscientious objectors (people

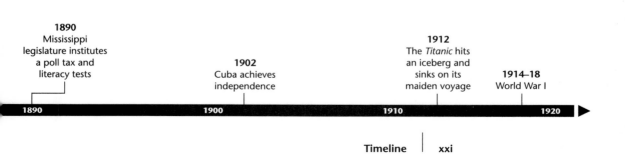

1890
Mississippi legislature institutes a poll tax and literacy tests

1902
Cuba achieves independence

1912
The *Titanic* hits an iceberg and sinks on its maiden voyage

1914–18
World War I

1890   1900   1910   1920

opposed to serving in wars) find alternative ways to serve the global community.

1917 The United States enters World War I (1914–18).

January 1919 Polish revolutionary political leader **Rosa Luxemburg** leads a failed worker rebellion in Berlin, Germany. She is captured and killed by the army.

March 1919 Journalist/activist **John Reed** publishes *Ten Days That Shook the World,* which wins acclaim as the finest eyewitness account of the Russian revolution.

April 1919 Mexican revolutionary **Emiliano Zapata** is assassinated by enemy troops.

December 1919 Russian-American Jewish anarchist **Emma Goldman** is expelled from the United States for her activities protesting U.S. involvement in World War I.

1920 The Nineteenth Amendment is passed, granting women the right to vote.

1925 **A. Philip Randolph** founds the Brotherhood of Sleeping Car Porters, the first black labor union in the United States.

1927–33 Rebel leader **Augusto Cesar Sandino** and his band of guerrilla fighters challenge the U.S. Marines for control of Nicaragua.

1930 **Mohandas Gandhi** leads his fellow Indians on a 240-mile "salt march" to the sea in defiance of British authorities.

1931 **Jane Addams** is awarded the Nobel Peace Prize.

1932 Educator and civil rights activist Myles Horton founds the **Highlander Research and Education Center,** the South's only integrated educational institution at the

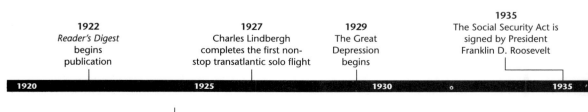

1922
Reader's Digest begins publication

1927
Charles Lindbergh completes the first non-stop transatlantic solo flight

1929
The Great Depression begins

1935
The Social Security Act is signed by President Franklin D. Roosevelt

1920   1925   1930   1935

time, in the Appalachian Mountains near Monteagle, Tennessee.

1935   Peace activist **Dorothy Day** founds the Catholic worker movement in New York.

1940   **Saul Alinsky,** a self-described "professional radical" from Chicago, founds the Industrial Areas Foundation for the training of community organizers.

1947   India achieves independence from Great Britain.

1950   Civil rights activist and performer **Paul Robeson**'s passport is revoked by the U.S. State Department and he is blacklisted by entertainment industry officials for his alleged communist sympathies.

1950   Civil rights activist and educator **Jo Ann Gibson Robinson** takes over as president of the Women's Political Committee (WPC). Under her leadership, the WPC lays the groundwork for the 1955–56 boycott of city buses by African Americans in Montgomery, Alabama.

1954   The Supreme Court, in *Brown v. Board of Education*, declares school segregation unconstitutional.

1955–56   Black residents of Montgomery, Alabama, stage a boycott of city buses, resulting in the racial integration of the buses.

1956   Civil rights activist **Robert F. Williams** takes over the Monroe, North Carolina, chapter of the National Association for the Advancement of Colored People (NAACP; founded in 1909) and arms its members so they can defend local African Americans against the Ku Klux Klan.

1957   Ghana becomes the first African nation to achieve independence from a colonial power and **Kwame Nkrumah** is named its first prime minister.

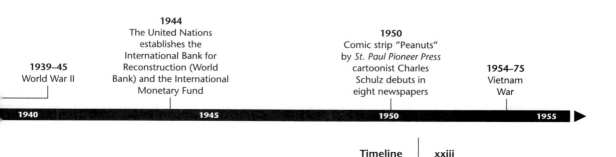

1939–45
World War II

1944
The United Nations establishes the International Bank for Reconstruction (World Bank) and the International Monetary Fund

1950
Comic strip "Peanuts" by *St. Paul Pioneer Press* cartoonist Charles Schulz debuts in eight newspapers

1954–75
Vietnam War

1940   1945   1950   1955

1959 U.S.-backed dictator Fulgencia Batista flees Cuba; Fidel Castro and **Ernesto "Ché" Guevara** lead triumphant rebel troops through the streets of Havana.

1960 The **Student Nonviolent Coordinating Committee** is founded in Raleigh, North Carolina.

1961 Medical doctor and revolutionary **Frantz Fanon** publishes *The Wretched of the Earth,* in which he advocates that colonized people violently overthrow their oppressors.

1961 **Amnesty International** is founded in England by lawyer Peter Benenson with the mission of freeing all "prisoners of conscience."

1962 Peace activist **Tom Hayden** authors "The Port Huron Statement," the political treatise defining the mission of the **Students for a Democratic Society.** The essay calls the American political establishment morally bankrupt and oppressive, and condemns militarism, materialism, and cultural conformity.

1962 Radical civil rights activist **Gloria Richardson** becomes cochair of the Cambridge Nonviolent Action Committee (CNAC). CNAC stages a militant, prolonged fight for the rights of African Americans in Cambridge, Maryland.

May 1963 Young activists of the "children's crusade" march for civil rights in Birmingham, Alabama, and are brutalized by the police.

August 1963 More than 250,000 people participate in the March on Washington for Jobs and Freedom. **Martin Luther King, Jr.,** delivers his "I Have a Dream" speech.

March 1964 Malcolm X forms the black nationalist group Organization of Afro-American Unity (OAAU).

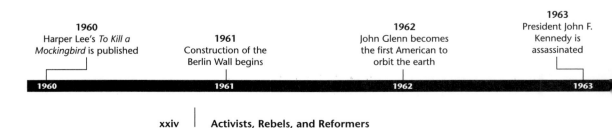

1960
Harper Lee's *To Kill a Mockingbird* is published

1961
Construction of the Berlin Wall begins

1962
John Glenn becomes the first American to orbit the earth

1963
President John F. Kennedy is assassinated

1960 1961 1962 1963

June 1964 One-thousand college-student volunteers descend on Mississippi for the beginning of Freedom Summer. They register voters, run freedom schools, and organize the Mississippi Freedom Democratic Party.

July 1964 President Lyndon B. Johnson signs the Civil Rights Act, thereby outlawing a variety of types of discrimination based on race, color, religion, or national origin.

October 1964 Student activist **Mario Savio** leads the Free Speech Movement on the campus of the University of California at Berkeley.

1965 The National Farm Workers Association, which changes its named to United Farm Workers in April 1966, is founded in Delano, California.

1965 Native American groups in the Pacific Northwest hold "fish-ins" to protest unconstitutional restrictions placed upon their fishing rights by state governments.

1965 Consumer advocate **Ralph Nader** publishes *Unsafe at Any Speed,* in which he criticizes General Motors for marketing the Corvair and other cars that he alleges the company knows to be unsafe.

February 21, 1965 Malcolm X is assassinated in Harlem, New York.

August 6, 1965 President Lyndon B. Johnson signs the Voting Rights Act, thereby outlawing all practices used to deny blacks the right to vote and empowering federal registrars to register black voters.

1966 The **Black Panther Party** is founded in Oakland, California.

October 1967 Countercultural activist **Abbie Hoffman** leads 75,000 people in a mass "exorcism of demons" at the

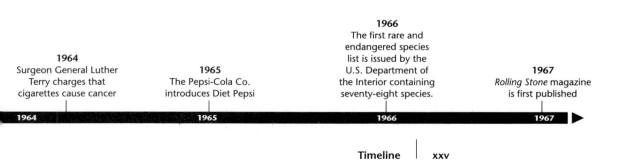

1964
Surgeon General Luther Terry charges that cigarettes cause cancer

1965
The Pepsi-Cola Co. introduces Diet Pepsi

1966
The first rare and endangered species list is issued by the U.S. Department of the Interior containing seventy-eight species.

1967
Rolling Stone magazine is first published

1964   1965   1966   1967

Pentagon in Washington, D.C., in protest of the Vietnam War (1954–75).

April 4, 1968 Martin Luther King, Jr., is assassinated in Memphis, Tennessee.

May 1968 Student activist **Daniel Cohn-Bendit** leads French students in a nationwide revolt.

May 1968 Daniel and Philip Berrigan and seven other peace activists use napalm to burn draft records at the Selective Service office in Catonsville, Maryland, in protest of the Vietnam War (1954–75).

July 1968 The **American Indian Movement** is founded in Minneapolis, Minnesota.

August 1968 Thousands of antiwar and antiracism protesters converge on the Democratic National Convention in Chicago. In what is later described as a "police riot," columns of police beat and tear-gas nonviolent demonstrators.

November 1969–June 1971 Indians of All Tribes occupies Alcatraz Island, San Francisco Bay, California, demanding it be returned to Native Americans.

December 4, 1969 Black Panther Party activists Fred Hampton and Mark Clark are shot to death by police in a pre-dawn raid on their Chicago apartment.

1970 Brazilian educator **Paulo Freire** publishes his most famous book, *Pedagogy of the Oppressed,* in which he outlines a teaching method for illiterate adults that encourages them to participate in the transformation of the society in which they live.

1971 Environmental scientist **Barry Commoner** publishes his best-selling book, *The Closing Circle,* in which he

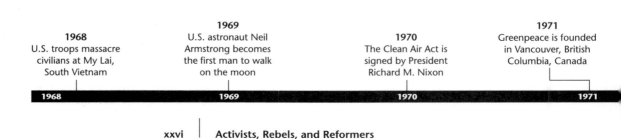

1968
U.S. troops massacre civilians at My Lai, South Vietnam

1969
U.S. astronaut Neil Armstrong becomes the first man to walk on the moon

1970
The Clean Air Act is signed by President Richard M. Nixon

1971
Greenpeace is founded in Vancouver, British Columbia, Canada

1968 | 1969 | 1970 | 1971

argues that technology has the potential to destroy human society.

1971 **Jesse Jackson** founds PUSH (People United to Serve Humanity) in Chicago.

June 1972 Radical activist **Angela Davis,** in one of the most closely watched trials in history, is acquitted of charges of kidnapping, conspiracy, and murder in connection with the attempted escape of a prisoner in California.

1972–73 Members of the **American Indian Movement** and other Native Americans occupy the village of Wounded Knee on the Pine Ridge Reservation in South Dakota in protest of the corrupt tribal government of chairman Dick Wilson.

1975 Mozambique wins independence from Portugal; **Samora Machel** becomes the new republic's first president.

1976 **Mairead Corrigan and Betty Williams** win the Nobel Peace Prize for their efforts to bring about peace in war-torn Northern Ireland.

1976 Civil rights activist **Unita Blackwell** is elected mayor of Mayersville, Mississippi, a town that had previously denied her the right to vote.

1978 **Lois Gibbs** becomes president of the Love Canal (New York) Homeowners Association, a group organized to fight for the cleanup of hazardous wastes that had been dumped at the site by Hooker Chemical Company in the 1940s.

July 1979 The Sandinista Front for National Liberation (known by the Spanish acronym FSLN, or Sandinistas) topples the U.S.-backed dictatorship in Nicaragua.

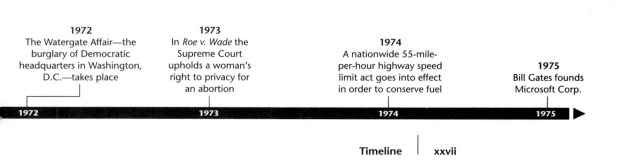

1972
The Watergate Affair—the burglary of Democratic headquarters in Washington, D.C.—takes place

1973
In *Roe v. Wade* the Supreme Court upholds a woman's right to privacy for an abortion

1974
A nationwide 55-mile-per-hour highway speed limit act goes into effect in order to conserve fuel

1975
Bill Gates founds Microsoft Corp.

1972 1973 1974 1975

March 24, 1980 Archbishop **Oscar Romero** of El Salvador, an outspoken critic of the violence committed by the armed forces in his country, is assassinated as he conducts mass.

1982 Egyptian feminist **Nawal El Saadawi** founds the Arab Women's Solidarity Association (AWSA), an international group of Arab women committed to "lifting the veil from the mind" of women.

1982 **Tom Hayden** is elected to the California State Assembly. He serves until 1991, at which time he is elected to the state senate. California's term limit law forced him to give up his state senate seat in 1999.

1983 The Women's Encampment for a Future of Peace and Justice protests nuclear arms at the Seneca Army Depot in Romulus, New York.

1985 The Indigenous Women's Network is founded by women representing three hundred Indian nations at a five-day conference at the Yelm, Washington, home of **Janet McCloud.**

1986 Native American activist **Winona LaDuke** founds the White Earth Land Recovery Project, the goal of which is to buy back or otherwise reclaim former Indian lands.

1988 Indigenous Malaysian **Harrison Ngau** is granted the Right Livelihood Award (considered the alternative Nobel Peace Prize) for his efforts to stop logging in the rainforest of Borneo.

1989 Radical feminist and author **Margaret Randall**'s U.S. citizenship is restored by the Immigration Appeals Board. The Immigration and Naturalization Service had denied Randall's citizenship and tried to deport her from the country in 1985 because her writings

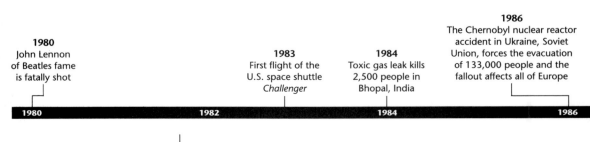

1980
John Lennon
of Beatles fame
is fatally shot

1983
First flight of the
U.S. space shuttle
Challenger

1984
Toxic gas leak kills
2,500 people in
Bhopal, India

1986
The Chernobyl nuclear reactor
accident in Ukraine, Soviet
Union, forces the evacuation
of 133,000 people and the
fallout affects all of Europe

1980   1982   1984   1986

were deemed to "advocate the economic, international and governmental doctrines of world communism."

1990 Israeli lawyer **Felicia Langer** quits her practice of defending Palestinian victims of human rights abuses and leaves the country, stating that justice for Palestinians is impossible in the Israeli military court system.

May 1990 A bomb explodes in the car of environmental activists **Judi Bari** and Darryl Cherney as they drive to a college campus to recruit volunteers for Redwood Summer (a summer-long demonstration against the logging of ancient redwoods). Bari is seriously injured; the case remains unsolved.

1991 **Aung San Suu Kyi** is awarded the Nobel Peace Prize for her efforts to bring democracy to Myanmar (Burma).

1991 **Patricia Ireland** takes over as president of the National Organization for Women (NOW).

1992 **Rigoberta Menchú** receives the Nobel Peace Prize for her work on behalf of social, political, and economic justice for Guatemalan Indians.

1992 Chinese émigré and former political prisoner **Harry Wu** founds the Laogai Foundation in the United States to educate Americans about human rights abuses in China and to advocate for reform.

1993 **Nelson Mandela** and South African President F. W. deKlerk are jointly awarded the Nobel Peace Prize for leading their nation down a nonviolent path toward democracy.

1993 Bangladeshi writer **Taslima Nasrin**'s first novel, *Shame*, is published, leading to calls for her death by Muslim fundamentalists.

1988
Internet virus jams over six thousand military computers

1989
Demolition of the Berlin Wall begins

1991
Operation Desert Storm to end the Persian Gulf War is launched

1994
Major League baseball players strike forces the cancellation of the World Series

1988   1990   1992   1994

1994 **Nelson Mandela** wins the presidency of South Africa in the country's first all-race elections.

1996 The passage of Proposition 209 in California ends that state's policy of affirmative action in government agencies.

1996 **Ralph Nader** and **Winona LaDuke** run for president and vice-president of the United States on the Green Party ticket. (Nader runs again in 2000.)

1997 Chinese pro-democracy activist **Wei Jingsheng** is freed and sent to the United States after spending seventeen years in prison in his native country.

March 4, 1999 Native American activist **Ingrid Washinawa-tok**, in Colombia to assist the U'wa people in their fight against oil drilling on their land, is killed by rebel soldiers.

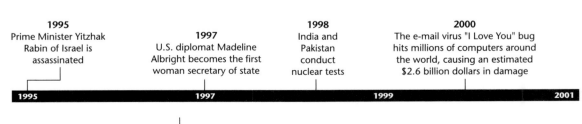

| **1995** | | **1998** | **2000** |
| Prime Minister Yitzhak Rabin of Israel is assassinated | **1997** U.S. diplomat Madeline Albright becomes the first woman secretary of state | India and Pakistan conduct nuclear tests | The e-mail virus "I Love You" bug hits millions of computers around the world, causing an estimated $2.6 billion dollars in damage |

| 1995 | 1997 | 1999 | 2001 |

Activists,
Rebels, and
Reformers

Ralph Nader

Born February 27, 1934
Winsted, Connecticut

Public interest lawyer and consumer advocate

R alph Nader began his public career in consumer protection in 1964, when he exposed safety flaws in automobile design during hearings in Washington, D.C. Since that time he has focused on the enforcement of workplace safety laws, the establishment of food and drug safety laws, environmental protection, auto insurance reform, and many other issues.

Beginning in 1969, with the Center for Study of Responsive Law, Nader has founded numerous public interest groups that carry out his agenda of consumer protection, worker safety, and environmentalism. A sampling of the organizations established by Nader and staffed by "Nader's Raiders" (young activists and lawyers who work for social change and accept low pay) includes the numerous statewide Public Interest Research Groups (PIRGs), Public Citizen, and the Project for Corporate Responsibility. Nader—a six-foot, four-inch tall bachelor who is now gray-haired—continues to work eighty hours a week.

Introduced to social justice issues as a child

Nader was the youngest of four children born to Lebanese immigrants Nathra and Rose Bouziane Nader. The

"Individuals still count. They can generate a momentum for change; they can challenge large and complex institutions; there still is a very critical role for citizen action and for the development of citizenship that will improve the quality of life in the country."

Ralph Nader in Ralph Nader: Crusader for Safe Consumer Products and Lawyer for the Public Interest.

Ralph Nader.
Courtesy of the Library of Congress.

395

Naders settled in Winsted, Connecticut, where they ran a successful Lebanese restaurant and bakery.

Social justice issues were frequent topics of conversation in the Nader home. At a young age Nader was taught to think critically about world affairs. His parents stressed the need to take action to rectify injustices. Nader grew up speaking both Arabic and English. He later learned Chinese, Russian, Spanish, and Portuguese.

Nader was an excellent student in the Winsted public schools. He particularly liked reading books by novelist Upton Sinclair (1878–1968) and others who brought to light social problems. (Sinclair's most famous work, *The Jungle,* was about the nightmarish working conditions in Chicago's [Illinois] meat-packing plants.)

Researches automobile safety in law school

After high school Nader attended Princeton University's Woodrow Wilson School of Public Affairs in Princeton, New Jersey. He graduated at the top of his class, then went on to Harvard Law School in Cambridge, Massachusetts. While in law school Nader researched issues of automobile safety. He had become interested in the topic after observing a number of tragic auto accidents during his months of hitchhiking around the United States. Nader wrote an extensive report on auto safety issues for a seminar in his final year at Harvard. He graduated from law school with distinction in 1958.

Begins law practice; teaches college courses

After law school Nader did not immediately begin practicing his chosen profession. Instead he enrolled in the army reserve. Nader spent six months on active duty at Fort Dix, in New Jersey, working as a chef. Upon completion of his duty, Nader became a freelance writer. He continued to pursue the question of automobile safety and in April 1959 published an article in *The Nation* titled "The Safe Car You Can't Buy."

Nader moved to Hartford, Connecticut, in 1959 and set up a law practice. Among his clients were people injured in car crashes. From 1961 to 1963, in addition to practicing law,

Nader Versus General Motors

Concurrent with the 1965 hearings on automobile safety (see below), Nader published his first book: *Unsafe at Any Speed*. In the book Nader criticized Detroit (Michigan) automobile manufacturers, principally General Motors, for marketing cars they knew to be unsafe. He charged that the automakers' desire for profit outweighed all other considerations. In the first chapter of his book, Nader focused on one car he believed to be particularly unsafe: the Corvair.

General Motors fought back against Nader's assertions—not by contesting the truthfulness of what he had written but by trying to discredit him personally. The company hired private detectives to trail Nader and interview his acquaintances, seeking to uncover unsavory details about Nader's personal life. The investigation turned up nothing—Nader was squeaky-clean.

When GM's harassment tactics were made public, it further tarnished the company's reputation. GM president James Roche apologized to Nader before Ribicoff's subcommittee (see below), while at the same time asserting that the company's investigation had been far less invasive than Nader had claimed. Nader sued GM for invasion of privacy and in 1970 was paid $425,000 by the company in an out-of-court settlement.

Unsafe at Any Speed sold many copies, and for a brief time made the bestseller list. Despite modifications made to the design of the Corvair, the negative publicity about the car caused sales to drop drastically. Production of the Corvair was discontinued in 1969.

Nader taught courses on history and political science at the University of Hartford, in Connecticut.

Takes on auto safety in Washington, D.C.

In 1964 Nader was hired by Daniel Patrick Moynihan, then assistant secretary of labor (under President Lyndon B. Johnson [1908–1973; president 1963–69]), as a highway safety consultant. Soon thereafter Nader offered his services to Senator Abraham Ribicoff, chairperson of the Senate Subcommittee on Executive Reorganization. Ribicoff's subcommittee was getting ready to hold hearings on automobile safety. Nader was hired to conduct background research and to give expert testimony at the hearings.

Nader (left) attracted a group of young followers, called Nader's Raiders, who were willing to work for causes he championed for little or no pay.
Reproduced by permission of Corbis Corporation.

Nader's testimony, along with some well-timed publicity, set the stage for passage of a strong National Traffic and Motor Vehicle Safety Act in September 1966. That Act had the effect of significantly changing automobile engineering practices.

Presses for meat-packaging regulations

After the flurry of automobile safety hearings had ended, Nader took on the meat-packing industry. He uncovered unsanitary practices that compromised the health of consumers. At Nader's urging, Congress adopted stringent meat-packaging regulations with the 1967 Wholesome Meat Act. Around the same time Nader drew attention to health hazards in mining, the dangers of gas pipelines, the injustices suffered by Native Americans, and the hazards associated with dental X rays.

Nader by that time had attracted a following among young activists, lawyers, students, and professionals. Like

Activists, Rebels, and Reformers

Nader, those individuals had a desire to make corporations and government bureaucracies responsive to the concerns of ordinary citizens. Also like Nader, they were willing to work long hours for virtually no pay. Most of those people, who became known as "Nader's Raiders," owed their ability to pay their own way while working for good causes to the support of their wealthy families. During the presidency of Jimmy Carter (1924–), from 1977 to 1981, many of Nader's Raiders won appointments to positions in government agencies.

Helps create government regulatory agencies

Throughout the 1970s Nader worked for the establishment of government agencies devoted to the rights of workers and consumers and the protection of the environment. Nader's lobbying led to the creation of the Occupational Safety and Health Administration (OSHA), the Environmental Protection Agency (EPA), and the Consumer Product Safety Commission (CPSC). In 1974 Nader's efforts were essential in the passage of the Freedom of Information Act (FOIA).

Faces challenge of conservative 1980s

During Ronald Reagan's (1911–) presidential administration, from 1981 to 1988, Nader witnessed the decline of the government agencies and regulations he had worked so hard to help create. Regulatory agency heads, who during the Carter years had passionately worked to advance their agencies' agendas, were replaced with bureaucrats intent on weakening their own agencies. Funding for regulatory operations was reduced. Legislation was passed that gutted the strength of consumer-protection and environmental laws.

During the 1980s Nader pushed for causes such as mandatory auto seatbelt use and the installation of air bags in cars. He also worked for restrictions on the production and use of chlorofluorocarbons (CFCs)—compounds that destroy the ozone layer. Nader was far less visible to the public in the 1980s, however, than he had been during the previous decade, because he devoted much time in the Reagan years to strengthening the many organizations he had created. In 1983, for example, he established USPIRG as an umbrella organization for the twenty-six state PIRGs.

The Organizational Network of Nader's Raiders

Nader has founded several organizations that carry out research and advocacy in the areas of consumer protection, government accountability, and environmentalism. The first of the Nader organizations, founded in 1969, was the Center for Study of Responsive Law (CSRL). The original staffers of the CSRL spent the summer of 1969 investigating the activities of the Interstate Commerce Commission and the Food and Drug Administration. They authored reports criticizing those government agencies for their inefficiency and ineffectiveness.

In 1970 Nader founded the Public Interest Research Group (PIRG), using money from his settlement with GM (see box "Nader versus General Motors"). The PIRG began as a group of lawyers in Washington, D.C., who investigated the safety of products and industries, petitioned for action by government agencies that regulated those industries, and lobbied Congress on legislative issues. The PIRG eventually expanded, with chapters being established in several states and on college campuses.

In 1971 Nader founded Public Citizen and became its first director. The original purpose of Public Citizen was to raise money to support the other Nader groups (up to that point, the groups had been funded by fees Nader received at speaking engagements). Public Citizen eventually split into two arms: one for fund-raising and the other for lobbying and legal action. Even after Nader officially resigned from his position with Public Citizen in 1980, the organization continued to push for traditional Nader issues. For example, Public Citizen has opposed the North American Free Trade Agreement (NAFTA; see information on NAFTA below), pressed for restrictions on dangerous pesticides, and lobbied for tougher labeling laws on foods and drugs.

Other "Nader-raider" groups include: Center for Auto Safety, Clean Water Action Project, Disability Rights Center, Pension Rights Center, and Project for Corporate Responsibility.

Opposes NAFTA

In the early 1990s Nader was among the most outspoken critics of the North American Free Trade Agreement (NAFTA). NAFTA—which in 1993 was narrowly ratified by Congress—created a common market between Canada, the United States, and Mexico. NAFTA's main supporters were U.S. business leaders. The reason for their support was that NAFTA facilitated the relocation of factories (in Spanish, *maquiladoras*) to Mexico, where labor costs one-seventh what it does in the United States.

Nader pointed out that the proposed agreement encouraged the exploitation of Mexican labor, the loss of U.S. jobs, and environmental degradation along the U.S.-Mexico border. Environmental damage had been evident even before the passage of NAFTA. For many years U.S. industrialists had been taking advantage of Mexico's lax environmental regulations, dumping hazardous chemical wastes into the Rio Grande. A report by the American Medical Association in 1991 characterized the border as "a virtual cesspool and breeding ground for infectious disease." Indeed, since NAFTA's passage alarming levels of lead and arsenic, as well as other toxic chemicals, have been found in the waters of the Rio Grande and on the beaches of southern California.

Nader was also on the winning end of policy debates in the 1990s. He supported California's victorious voter-referendum that rolled back car insurance rates 20 percent. Nader also successfully campaigned to defeat the proposed 50 percent pay hike for members of Congress.

Runs for president

Nader has launched two half-hearted campaigns for the presidency of the United States: in 1992 and in 1996. Nader's 1992 bid was limited to New Hampshire, where he ran a write-in campaign. Nader explained that he was not actually trying to win the presidency, but was giving voters a chance to express their dissatisfaction with the candidates offered by the Republicans and Democrats—George Bush (1924–; president 1989–1993) and Bill Clinton (1946–; president 1993–2001). Nader also suggested that the option "none of the above" be placed on ballots along with candidates' names.

In 1996 Nader accepted the Green Party's nomination for president. (The Green Party is a political organization that promotes environmentalism, women's rights, and workers' rights.) Nader refused to accept campaign contributions, spent only $5 thousand of his own money, and did very little campaigning. Nonetheless, Nader's name appeared on the ballot in thirty states. He and his vice-presidential running mate, Native

American activist **Winona LaDuke** (see entry), won seven hundred thousand votes (approximately 2 percent of the votes that were cast in those thirty states). In 2000 Nader ran again for president on the Green Party ticket launching his most serious campaign to date.

Sources

Books

Buckthorn, Robert F. *Nader: The People's Lawyer.* Englewood Cliffs, NJ: Prentice-Hall, Inc., 1972.

Gorey, Hays. *Nader and the Power of Everyman.* New York: Grosset & Dunlap, 1975.

McCarry, Charles. *Citizen Nader.* New York: Saturday Review Press, 1972.

Nader, Ralph, and Wesley L. Smith. *No Contest: Corporate Lawyers and the Perversion of Justice in America.* New York: Random House, 1996.

Peduzzi, Kelli. *Ralph Nader: Crusader for Safe Consumer Products and Lawyer for the Public Interest.* Milwaukee: Gareth Stevens Children's Books, 1990.

Articles

Durkin, Tish. "The Un-Candidate." *New York Times.* October 20, 1996.

Elvin, John. "Another Whirl-a-Gig Beanie in the Ring." *Insight on the News.* January 10, 2000: 34.

McCaslin, John. "Inside the Beltway." *Washington Times.* January 17, 2000: 6.

McGinn, Chris, and Michael McCauley. "Bush Administration Opens Backdoor to Gut Health, Safety Standards Via Trade Pact." *Public Citizen.* September/October 1992: 14–17.

Web Sites

Saldana, Lori/Sierra Club (San Diego chapter). "The Downside of the Border Boom." [Online] Available http://www.sierraclub.org/trade/SAL-DANA.HTML (accessed March 31, 1999).

Taslima Nasrin

**Born August 25, 1962
Mymensingh, Bangladesh**

**Writer, women's rights activist, poet,
and medical doctor**

Taslima Nasrin came into the public eye in 1993, when she published a novel criticizing the religious laws of her homeland, Bangladesh, and advocating equal rights for women. The following year Nasrin stated in a newspaper interview that the Koran (the holy book of the Muslim religion) should be revised. Despite her claim that she was misquoted, Islamic fundamentalists called for her death. Nasrin was forced to flee her home in Bangladesh and was given asylum in Sweden. She has become an international symbol of the intolerance of religious fundamentalism.

Conservative upbringing

Nasrin was born in 1962 in Mymensingh, Bangladesh (at that time, East Pakistan; Bangladesh gained its independence in 1971). She was raised in a very conservative area of what is one of the poorest and most densely populated countries in the world. Nasrin's father, Rojab Ali, was a medical doctor working for the government, and her mother, Eudalara, was a devoutly religious woman. Nasrin has at least two siblings, but other details of her childhood remain sketchy.

"I write against the religion because if women want to live like human beings, they will have to live outside of the religion and Islamic law."

Taslima Nasrin, 1994 television interview

Taslima Nasrin.
Reproduced by permission of AP/Wide World Photos.

At the age of nine Nasrin witnessed the violent revolt in the former East Pakistan that led to the creation of Bangladesh. Her parents' home was destroyed by Pakistani forces. Her father was tortured, and two of her uncles were killed. Her aunt was held prisoner by soldiers for sixteen days, during which time she was raped by ten men (the aunt later hanged herself). "My childhood memories are full of this war and painful, bloody birth of the new nation," Nasrin wrote in 1994.

After completing high school, Nasrin entered the Mymensingh Medical College. She earned her medical degree (with a specialty in anesthesiology) and in 1990 was assigned to a position as a gynecologist (a doctor specializing in women's medicine) at a small hospital in the nation's capital, Dhaka.

Writes criticisms of Islamic society

While practicing medicine, Nasrin continued the tradition of writing poetry she had begun as a child. She published several volumes of poetry, then started writing a syndicated (distributed for publication in numerous journals) newspaper column. Her articles focused on religious intolerance and the oppression of women in Muslim society. She also wrote books of fiction.

Over time Nasrin's writing became more militant. Inspired by the stories of abuse told by her patients and the reports of stonings of women accused of adultery, Nasrin railed against the rules of Islam, as well as men in general. Her writing also took on more explicitly sexual themes—a subject considered taboo in a conservative culture.

Before long, Nasrin found her freedom of expression restricted. In early 1992 groups of Islamic faithfuls led by mullahs (Islamic religious and political leaders) began attacking bookstores that carried Nasrin's writings. Nasrin was physically assaulted at a book fair but was not seriously hurt.

Publishes book, faces reprisals

Undeterred by the reaction of religious fundamentalists, Nasrin continued her literary crusade. In 1992, after receiving an award for her writings by the Indian state of West Bengal, Nasrin began work on a novel, *Shame*. In that book she criticized many aspects of Islamic society, including Muslims' treatment of Hindus (the religious majority in India, but minority in Bangladesh) and the sexual abuse of women. Nasrin's novel was published in February 1993, just three months after the destruction of an ancient Muslim mosque in northern India by Hindu extremists, and the retaliation by Muslim mobs against Hindus throughout India and Bangladesh.

"'Shame,' in fact, is shame to our country, shame to our government, shame to our society, shame to myself," stated Nasrin in a 1994 article. "For we have all deviated from our national ideal. We have all deviated from the humanism of man."

The Bangladeshi government responded to the publication of *Shame* by banning the book and revoking Nasrin's passport. The religious community reacted even more forcefully. A group of Muslim fundamentalists, called the Soldiers of Islam, issued a *fatwa* (holy judgment) calling for Nasrin's death and placed a $1,250 bounty on her head (it was later upped to $6,500). The fatwa was to be taken seriously. One newspaper in Bangladesh reported that between the nation's founding in 1971 through mid-1994, there had been five hundred cases of fatwa, and fifty women had been killed as a result. (Virtually every fatwa had been issued against poor rural women who were attempting to obtain some form of economic or social independence.)

Shame

Taslima Nasrin's first novel, *Shame* (in Arabic *Lajja*), was released in Bengali (the language spoken in Bangladesh and in northeastern India) in February 1993 and in English in 1997. *Shame* tells the story of the Duttas—a family of Bangladeshi Hindus caught up in a wave of anti-Hindu terror. It is a fictional tale set in the context of historically accurate events. The book became a rallying point for Hindus protesting Muslim oppression and raised the ire of Muslim fundamentalists in Bangladesh.

Shame owed its commercial success mostly to the controversy it created. As a literary work, however, *Shame* has received mediocre reviews. "A seething indictment of oppression and religious fundamentalism couched precariously as a novel," wrote a reviewer in *Library Journal*, "this important work is impassioned but difficult to read. More reportage and protest than story, it is recommended more for its historic than its literary value."

International organizations take her side

As word spread throughout the world of Nasrin's persecution in Bangladesh, foreign governments and organizations sought to protect her. The writers' group International PEN publicized Nasrin's plight and campaigned for her safety, as did famous writers Allen Ginsberg, Gunter Grass, John Irving, Norman Mailer, Amy Tan, Mario Vargas Llosa, and Salman Rushdie. Human rights groups **Amnesty International** (see entry) and the International Humanist and Ethical Union also came to Nasrin's defense.

Formal complaints filed by the governments of the United States, France, Sweden, and other nations prompted the Bangladeshi government to return Nasrin's passport. Despite the efforts of western governments and organizations, however, the fatwa against Nasrin remained.

Nasrin's words prompt general strike

Tensions in Bangladesh escalated in the fall of 1993, as the Soldiers of Islam intensified their efforts to kill Nasrin. Nasrin went to the police on October 6 seeking a protective order. Although the police chief issued the order, officers refused to honor it.

On October 10 the Soldiers of Islam held a general strike in the city of Sylhet, demanding Nasrin's death. A similar rally held on November 29 at the National Mosque in Dhaka drew ten thousand Muslim devotees. A counterdemonstration, supporting Nasrin and religious freedom, was held by one hundred women in Dhaka on December 16.

"Women, especially in the Islamic countries, are being exposed to loathsome male chauvinism," stated Nasrin in an interview published in *World Press Review* magazine in January 1994. "We are being used as a sex commodity on the pretext of religion. And the offenders have social and political sanction. If you protest against these malpractices, you will be dubbed a witch or a nymphomaniac."

Quote about Koran intensifies passions

After a relatively quiet spell, tensions between Nasrin and Muslim clerics reignited. The source of the controversy was a quote by Nasrin reported in *The Statesman*, a daily newspaper in Calcutta, India. The June 4, 1994, report said that Nasrin had commented that the Koran (the holy book considered by Muslims to be the literal word of God) should be "revised thoroughly."

Nasrin, for her part, claimed that she had been misquoted. She said that she had not criticized the Koran but Islamic law, called Sharia. "I asked for changes in the Sharia law to ensure equal rights for men and women," Nasrin explained. Her account was backed up by a second journalist present at the interview.

Nasrin's protestations were of no significance to her enemies. According to biographers Kathlyn and Martin Gay, new fatwas were issued for Nasrin's death, and the bounty on her head was increased. Two-hundred-thousand people protested in the streets of Dhaka, chanting "Hang her, hang her!" One speaker said about Nasrin, "She is a reincarnation of the devil and does not deserve to keep her head." Another speaker argued, "She has committed an unforgivable crime and must pay for it dearly."

Goes into hiding

On July 1, Muslim clerics held a general strike to protest Nasrin's alleged attack on Islam. They threatened to set loose thousands of poisonous snakes in the capital if Nasrin was not executed. An order for Nasrin's arrest on charges of "insulting religion or religious beliefs" was issued by the government. Fearing for her life, Nasrin went into hiding.

The fact that Nasrin had been married and divorced three times by the age of thirty-one, and had referred to marriage as "bonded slavery in most cases," did not help her cause, (Nasrin alleges that her husbands beat her) nor did her short, tradition-defying haircut.

From her hideout, Nasrin consented to an interview with an Australian television crew. "Our religion doesn't give women any human dignity," Nasrin stated. "I write against the religion because if women want to live like human beings, they will have to live outside of the religion and Islamic law."

Seeks refuge in Sweden

On July 15, 1994, Nasrin appeared on a news report of the British Broadcasting Corporation, asking Amnesty International for assistance. Three weeks later the human rights organization helped Nasrin slip out of the country, disguised as a veiled Muslim woman, to an undisclosed location in Sweden. That August Nasrin won a writing award from the International PEN Club.

From her new home, Nasrin granted an interview with the *New Yorker* magazine. "This is the first time ever, in the history of Bangladesh, that the fundamentalists have been able to unite 300,000 people on one issue—the need for my death. If they kill me, okay, but what about the future of Bangladesh? They'll kill all progressive forces, all progressive thought. All enlightenment will stop."

Nasrin again denied the quote about the Koran that had gotten her into trouble that June. "I said that Shariat law should be revised," stated Nasrin. "I want a modern, civilized law, where women are given equal rights. I want no religious law that discriminates . . . no Hindu law, no Christian law, no Islamic law. Why should a man be entitled to have four wives? Why should a son get two-thirds of his parents' property when a daughter can inherit only a third? Should I be killed for saying this?"

On October 17, Bangladeshi prosecutors issued a court order for Nasrin to stand trial on charges of blasphemy.

Returns home to care for ailing mother

For four years after leaving Bangladesh, Nasrin lived in Sweden, Germany, and the United States. In September 1998 Nasrin returned home to care for her mother, who was dying of cancer. During her four months in the country, she stayed in a different house every night to avoid being captured. John Stackhouse, writing for Toronto's *Globe and Mail* newspaper, reported that Nasrin was "wanted by police who vow to put her on trial, hunted by religious extremists who want to kill her, and shunned by feminists who would rather she just fade away." (Some Bangladeshi feminists accused Nasrin of having no popular base of support, but having created a national frenzy using the international media.)

That November Nasrin was ordered to turn herself in to authorities by January 5, 1999, to stand trial on charges of blasphemy (criticizing God or religion). Her penalty, if convicted, would have been up to three years in jail. At the same time, Bangladeshi religious leaders renewed their call for Nasrin's execution and threatened to topple the government if police offered Nasrin protection.

Flees from death threats again

Nasrin's mother died on January 11, 1999. Two weeks later, Nasrin made another dramatic escape from her homeland. With the assistance of the European Union's ambassador to Bangladesh, Nasrin was transported back to Sweden. "I feel safe and at the same time I feel so empty because of not having a loving mother," Nasrin stated in an interview published in the Spring 1999 edition of *Free Inquiry* magazine—an international human-rights journal of which Nasrin is an editor.

Nasrin claims to speak for the interests of the 85 percent of Bangladeshi women who are illiterate. "My purpose was not to shock," Nasrin stated in a 1995 interview in *Maclean's*. "I just wrote what I feel. My anger, my tears. . . . I don't think I'm a great philosopher, political leader or writer. I was a medical doctor writing to express myself. I don't think that I should be killed for it."

Sources

Books

Gay, Kathlyn, and Martin K. Gay. *Heroes of Conscience: A Biographical Dictionary.* Santa Barbara, CA: ABC-CLIO, 1996, pp. 280–81.

Goodwin, Jan. *Price of Honor: Muslim Women Lift the Veil of Silence on the Islamic World.* Boston: Little, Brown & Co., 1994.

Articles

Bhattacharya, Pallab. "A Rushdie in Bangladesh." *World Press Review.* January 1994: 49.

Cherry, Matt. "Taslima Nasrin Escapes Bangladesh." *Free Inquiry.* Spring 1999: 14.

"Dhaka: Author Taslima Nasrin Faces Blasphemy Charges." *Time International.* November 16, 1998: 22.

Douglas, Carol Anne. "Bangladesh: Feminist Writer Faces Threats." *Off Our Backs.* November 1998: 3.

Edwords, Frederick. "In Defense of Taslima Nasrin." *The Humanist.* September-October 1994: 42+.

Ingraham, Janet. Review of "Shame." *Library Journal.* November 1, 1997: 117.

Morris, Nomi. "Fighting Words: A Poet Forced into Hiding by Muslim Extremists Still Speaks Out for Oppressed Women." *Maclean's.* October 9, 1995: 44.

Shabad, Steven. "Poetic Injustice." *World Press Review.* January 1998: 21.

Shamsul, S. M. "Women in the Era of Modernity and Islamic Fundamentalism." *Signs: Journal of Women in Culture and Society.* 1998: 429–61.

Walsh, James. "Death to the Author." *Time.* August 15, 1994: 26–27.

Weaver, Mary Anne. "A Fugitive from Injustice." *New Yorker.* September 12, 1994: 70–28.

Harrison Ngau

Born 1960
Sarawak, Malaysia

**Native Malaysian environmentalist
and indigenous rights activist**

In the late 1970s Harrison Ngau joined the movement opposed to logging in the rainforest on his native island of Borneo. In the 1980s he formed a chapter of Friends of the Earth and drew world attention to the plight of Borneo's indigenous groups, who were being driven out of their ancestral homelands by logging. Ngau organized the rainforest dwellers to resist the timber companies' equipment, with their bodies if necessary. In 1990 Ngau won a seat in the Malaysian parliament and successfully campaigned for a law protecting tribal lands in his home state of Sarawak.

Raised in traditional community

Ngau (pronounced ngo; the "ng" sounds like the end of "song") was born in the state of Sarawak, Malaysia, on the northern portion of the island of Borneo (Borneo is divided among the countries of Malaysia, Indonesia, and Brunei). He was raised in a tribal Kayan community on the River Baram and lived in a multifamily dwelling called a "longhouse." Ngau's family, like their ancestors before them, survived by hunting and farming in the rainforest. The rainforest held everything

Ngau, a native Kayan environmental activist, has made it his life's work to protect the trees and indigenous communities of the Borneo rainforest.

Harrison Ngau.
Reproduced by permission of Archive Photos.

The Plunder of Borneo's Natural Resources

Borneo is the third-largest island in the world and is largely covered by tropical rainforest. Sitting in the South China Sea in Southeast Asia, Borneo—divided among the nations of Malaysia, Indonesia, and Brunei—is home to several tribes of rainforest-dwelling indigenous people. For millennia those people have lived a hunter-and-gatherer lifestyle, relying on the rainforest to provide for all their needs of food and shelter. In the mid-twentieth century, however, multinational timber companies began cutting trees on the edges of the island. Since that time, the world of Borneo's native inhabitants has been turned upside-down.

In the early 1970s, with the coastal rainforest decimated, logging companies gained approval from governments or tribal leaders (whom they bribed with money and alcohol) and headed into the island's interior. The companies clear cut huge tracts of ancient tropical forest, then abandoned the areas—leaving behind polluted, eroded wastelands. In Sarawak state, which occupies the northwestern portion of Borneo, 30 percent of the territory was logged between 1963 and 1985. (During those years, Malaysia was providing some 50 percent of the world's total log exports.) As the timber trucks moved in, indigenous peoples were forcibly relocated.

In the 1970s indigenous people began to stand up to the timber companies. They managed to slow the pace of rainforest destruction over the next two decades by blocking logging trucks with their bodies and launching legal battles. The timber companies, while continuing to inch their way through Borneo, have also been logging in forests in China, Africa, and South America.

that the Kayan people, as well as the state's other indigenous inhabitants—the Kelabit and Penan people—needed to survive.

Ngau was among the first generation of Kayans to leave the village and attend school in the town of Marudi. Upon completing secondary school, Ngau found a job with an oil prospecting company in the coastal town of Miri.

Becomes active in fight against logging

In the late 1970s, while Ngau was working for the oil company, logging companies—previously positioned on the outskirts of Borneo—began working their way inland (see box

"The Plunder of Borneo's Natural Resources"). Ngau became alarmed at the environmental destruction and the impact of logging on indigenous communities—particularly as the government was forcibly relocating communities that lay in the path of the loggers. Ngau joined a small antilogging coalition comprised of Kayan, Penan, and Kelabit people fighting to retain their way of life.

Ngau became recognized as an effective environmental advocate. In 1982 he was asked to found and head a chapter of Friends of the Earth (known by the initials for its name in Malay, SAM) in Sarawak. Ngau attracted large numbers of indigenous people to his organization. He initiated petition drives and letter-writing campaigns to halt the logging and worked to expose the links between timber company executives and the corrupt government officials. Perhaps most importantly, Ngau established a communication network among the widely dispersed rainforest communities and united native people in the fight against logging.

Blocks logging roads

In 1983, when logging in Sarawak reached its peak of 75 acres cleared per hour (providing 39 percent of Malaysia's tropical log exports), Ngau and his allies decided it was time to put their bodies on the line. Borrowing a tactic from the environmental group Greenpeace, rainforest defenders set up blockades on the roads surrounding logging camps. The activists continued to blockade camps through the early 1990s, bringing much of the logging to a halt. Many of them were arrested for their actions.

In 1987 Ngau led a delegation of indigenous leaders (clad in their tribal clothing) to the Malaysian capital of Kuala Lumpur for talks with government officials. Although the talks yielded no agreements, they did publicize the destruction of tribal communities to domestic and international constituencies.

Also in the 1980s Ngau conducted research into the leadership of the logging companies. He discovered that one of the largest companies, the Limbang Trading Company, was owned by Malaysia's minister of environment and tourism. Ngau spread the news of this government corruption to Malaysia's international trading partners, much to the embar-

Burnum Burnum and the Fight for Australian Aboriginal Rights

Burnum Burnum was born Henry Penrith in January 1936 in Wallaga Lake, an aboriginal community on the south coast of New South Wales, Australia. (Aboriginal people, or Aborigines, are the native people of Australia. Their culture thrived for forty thousand years but went into rapid decline after the arrival of the British in 1788.) Burnum's mother died when he was a young child. He was then taken from his father and placed in an orphanage, making him part of Australia's "stolen generation."

The stolen generation in Australia consisted of some one hundred thousand mixed-race (white-and-aboriginal) children who were taken from their homes between 1910 and the early 1970s and raised in institutions in accordance with white customs and lifestyles. The point of that ill-fated government initiative was to eliminate aboriginal culture by assimilating mixed-race people while letting small aboriginal communities in the interior of the country die out.

Despite suffering beatings and other forms of humiliation in the orphanage, Burnum excelled in academics and sports. After finishing school he spent thirteen years working for the Agriculture Department in the state of New South Wales.

In the mid-1960s Burnum experienced an awakening of his aboriginal heritage. He changed his named to Burnum Burnum, which means "great warrior," after his great-grandfather, who was a warrior from the Wurundjeri tribe. He spoke out on behalf of aboriginal rights and with other Aborigines organized demonstrations for native people's rights. Largely due to the efforts of Burnum, a national referendum held in 1967 gave Australia's 300,000 Aborigines the right to vote and other civil rights.

rassment of Malaysian leaders. Ngau was vilified by timber cutters and their government allies, and found himself the target of a campaign of harassment.

Jailed without charge

In October 1987 police broke down blockades in the rainforest and arrested Ngau and some forty tribal activists. Under Malaysia's Internal Security Act the government (in violation of international human rights standards) can detain sus-

Burnum Burnum. *Reproduced by permission of Archive Photos.*

In the 1970s Burnum campaigned for the burial of aboriginal skeletal remains being displayed at the Museum of Tasmania. The bones purportedly belonged to the last full-blooded Aborigine woman in Tasmania, who died in the 1890s. The museum finally released the remains in 1976.

In 1988 Burnum captured international headlines when, during the celebrations of Australia's bicentennial (the two hundredth anniversary of the English settlers' arrival—or invasion, as Burnum regarded it—in Australia), he traveled to England and symbolically laid claim to that land for Australia's aboriginal people. Burnum's trip involved climbing the hills of Dover and planting the aboriginal flag. A sarcastic reference of Burnum's regarding the stated British intentions toward the Aborigines was quoted in his obituary in *The Independent* (London), "We wish no harm to England's native people. We are here to bring you good manners, refinement and an opportunity to make a Koompartoo, a fresh start."

Burnum died of a heart attack on August 17, 1997, in Sydney. He was sixty-one years old.

pects without charge for up to two months. In Ngau's case, his sixty days were served in solitary confinement and he was never charged with any crime. At the end of that time Ngau was released but placed under house arrest. For the next two years he was not allowed to leave his home after dark.

Funds electoral campaign with award money

In 1988 Ngau was a corecipient of the Right Livelihood Award (considered the alternative Nobel Peace Prize). He shared the $100 thousand prize with the Malaysian Friends of the Earth organization and that group's founder, Mohamed Idris. In 1990 Ngau was awarded the Goldman Environmental Prize by an American foundation that recognized the environmental efforts of six individuals—one from each of six continents.

Ngau used the $60 thousand Goldman Prize money to finance an electoral campaign for a seat in the Malaysian national parliament. In the fall of 1990 he won the race against his timber-industry-backed opponent. As a lawmaker Ngau continued to champion the interests of the rainforest people. His efforts bore fruit in 1993 when the parliament passed a law giving priority to the needs of rainforest tribal peoples over logging companies in the state of Sarawak.

Rainforest fight continues

As Ngau and his supporters learned, legislation slowed the logging but did not bring it to a halt. People had to remain ready to erect new blockades when necessary. Ngau left the parliament in 1995 after serving one term and returned to the rainforest. There he continues to work with the Sarawak Friends of the Earth to protect the land and livelihood of the rainforest dwellers.

Sources

Books

Bevis, William W. *Borneo Log: The Struggle for Sarawak's Forests.* Seattle: University of Washington Press, 1995.

Button, John. *The Radicalism Handbook: A Complete Guide to the Radical Movement in the Twentieth Century.* London, England: Cassell, 1995, p. 260.

"Harrison Ngau." *Contemporary Heroes and Heroines.* Vol. 3. Edited by Terrie M. Rooney. Detroit: Gale Research, Inc., 1998.

Articles

"Aborigine Stakes Claim to England." *Toronto Star.* January 27, 1988: A3.

Anderson, Susan Heller. "Chronicle." *New York Times.* April 17, 1990: B10.

"Defenders of the Planet." *Time.* April 23, 1990: 78+.

Farnsworth, Clyde H. "Burnum Burnum, 61, Fighter for Australia's Aborigines" (Obituary). *New York Times.* August 20, 1997: D20.

Maniam, Hari S. "Widening Ring of Arrests Spreads to Borneo State." *Associated Press.* October 30, 1987.

Milliken, Robert. "Obituary: Burnum Burnum." *The Independent* (London). August 20, 1997: 11.

"Much Done and More to Do; A Malaysian Activist Prepares His Next Move." *Asiaweek.* November 3, 1995: 9.

Web Sites

"The Borneo Project." Earth Island Institute. [Online] Available http://www.earthisland.org/berkborn/bri.html (accessed March 15, 2000).

Brunton, Ron. "Give the Man a Break." *Herald Sun* (Australia). [Online] Available http://ipa.org.au/Media/rbhs220798.html (accessed March 15, 2000).

"Sahabat Alam Malaysia—Sarawak (1988)." The Right Livelihood Award. [Online] Available http://www.rightlivelihood.se/recip1988_4.html.

Kwame Nkrumah

Born September 21, 1909
Nkroful, Ghana (formerly Gold Coast)
Died April 27, 1972
Bucharest, Romania

Independence leader and first president of Ghana

"Only the unified movement of the colonial people, determined to assert its right to independence, can compel any colonial power to lay down its 'white man's burden,' which rests so heavily upon the shoulders of the so-called 'backward' peoples, who have been subjugated, humiliated, robbed, and degraded to the level of cattle."

Kwame Nkrumah.
Public Domain.

Kwame Nkrumah led his nation, Ghana, to independence from Great Britain in 1957. Ghana was the first African nation to break free from colonialism (the policy by which one nation exerts control over another nation or territory) and served as an inspiration to the rest of the continent. Nkrumah also championed the unification of West Africa into a United States of Africa. He served as prime minister of Ghana (formerly called the Gold Coast), during a period of limited self-rule, from 1952 to 1957. Following Ghana's independence in 1957, Nkrumah served as the new republic's first prime minister until his overthrow in a military coup in 1966. Nkrumah was the first internationally recognized black African statesman and continues to serve as a symbol of African self-sufficiency and unity.

Raised in large family

Kwame Nkrumah (pronounced KWAH-me en-KROO-muh) was born around September 21, 1909, in the village of Nkroful (his exact birth date is not known since birth records were not kept in his village). While his christened name was Francis Nwia Kofi, he preferred his tribal name, Kwame.

At the time Nkrumah was born, his country was a colony of Great Britain and was called the Gold Coast. The country was named for its great reserves of gold, bauxite, diamonds, and other precious metals and minerals. Great Britain had taken over the economic and political governance of the country in 1874.

Nkrumah was his mother's only child. He was raised in a large family, however, because his father had several wives (in keeping with village customs of the day) and Nkrumah had many stepbrothers and stepsisters. Nkrumah grew up in a rural village, in the vicinity of the ocean. He enjoyed spending long periods of time alone, enjoying the natural surroundings.

Shows aptitude for learning and teaching

Nkrumah attended Roman Catholic mission schools and did very well in his studies. At the age of seventeen he worked as a student teacher at a local school. The next year he was recruited to attend the Government Training College in the capital of Accra. There Nkrumah met people advocating the liberation of African nations from foreign rule. He began to develop his own theories of national emancipation, which involved blacks and whites working together.

Nkrumah graduated from college in 1930 and spent the next five years working as a schoolteacher. He became restless, however, and sought ways to further his own education.

Receives university education in the United States

Nkrumah was encouraged by a former mentor to go to college in the United States. In 1935 he applied, and was accepted, to Lincoln University. Located in Pennsylvania, Lincoln University was the first institute of higher learning in the United States that was open to blacks.

Nkrumah graduated from Lincoln in 1939 with degrees in economics and sociology; he then enrolled in Lincoln Theological Seminary. At the same time, he taught philosophy to undergraduates at Lincoln and took education classes at the University of Pennsylvania (U-Penn). In 1942 Nkrumah graduated with a master's degree in education from U-Penn and a bachelor's degree in theology from Lincoln Theological Seminary. The following year he earned a master's degree in philosophy from U-Penn. He continued teaching at Lincoln University through 1945.

Political awakenings

During his ten years in the United States, Nkrumah read the works of revolutionary thinkers such as **Karl Marx** (1818–1883; German economist and father of communist theory; see entry) and John Stuart Mill (1806–1873; English social reformer). He also studied the teachings of black nationalist leader Marcus Garvey (1887–1940). Garvey preached pride in black African heritage and the need for African Americans and Africans to achieve political and economic self-sufficiency; he also advocated that African Americans return to Africa.

Nkrumah also learned first-hand about racial discrimination in the pre-civil rights United States. He wrote of his own degrading experience at a whites-only facility: "I was parched with thirst, and I entered the refreshment room and asked the white American waiter if I could have a drink of water. He frowned and looked down on me as if I were something unclean. 'The place for you, my man, is the spittoon outside,' he declared as he dismissed me from his gaze. I was so shocked that I could not move."

Joins Pan-African movement in Europe

In 1945 Nkrumah traveled to England, intending to further his education at the London School of Economics. Instead, he became increasingly involved in the African independence movement and devoted his time to political organizing and writing. Nkrumah joined Pan-Africanist groups in London (Pan-Africanism is the political theory favoring an independent Africa and political unity among people of African descent), including the West African National Secretariat—of which he became general secretary. The Secretariat, in its newspaper *The New Africa,* called for the liberation of west African nations under British or French control. During his two years in England, Nkrumah rose to international fame as a leading proponent of African independence.

At the Fifth Pan-African Conference, held in London in October 1945, Nkrumah declared: "All colonies must be free from foreign imperialist control, whether political or economic. The people of the colonies must have the right to elect their own government, a government without restrictions from a foreign power. We say to the peoples of the colonies that they must strive for these ends by all means at their disposal."

Called back to Ghana

Nkrumah was called back to his country in 1947 by organizers of the United Gold Coast Convention (UGCC). The UGCC, a politically moderate organization of Ghana's elite and educated black populace, advocated limited self-rule for Ghana. At the time, Ghana was facing an economic crisis because Great Britain's policy regarding Ghana's principle export crop, cocoa, was resulting in high inflation and low wages. UGCC organizers believed that the time was ripe for change in Ghana and that Nkrumah would be capable of unifying the populace around their demands. Nkrumah, upon his return to his homeland, was made general secretary of the UGCC.

Founds Convention People's Party

Nkrumah grew increasingly dissatisfied with the policies of the UGCC founders. He felt they were too conservative in their approach and too closely connected with the interests of the British rulers. Thus in 1949 Nkrumah left the UGCC and formed his own organization, the Convention People's Party (CPP). The CPP had as its goal complete independence from Great Britain, the installation of a democratic government, solidarity of Ghanaians across ethnic and religious lines, and a unified, independent West Africa.

The CPP attracted many members away from the floundering UGCC and quickly became the colony's leading political force. Under Nkrumah's leadership, the CPP instituted a program of nonviolent resistance, holding national strikes to protest British rule. Nkrumah himself was imprisoned for several months in 1950, during which the British authorities consented to a limited system of self-governance for Ghana. In elections held in February 1951, Nkrumah's CPP won thirty-three of the thirty-eight legislative assembly seats. Nkrumah, who was elected to be the leader of government business (the highest elected office), was released from prison to take his seat.

Works for independence

Throughout the 1950s Nkrumah worked with British authorities to arrange a gradual pullout of British forces. He undertook a difficult balancing act, maintaining trusting, respectful relationships with both British colonialists and his native constituents (who were pushing for independence).

In 1952 Nkrumah's title was changed to prime minister of the legislative assembly. The following year he called upon the British to set a date for independence. In his July 10, 1953, address, known as his "Motion of Destiny" speech, Nkrumah stated, "there comes a time in the history of all colonial peoples when they must, because of their will to throw off the hampering shackles of colonialism, boldly assert their God-given right to be free of a foreign ruler." After three more years of an uneasy peace, Great Britain announced that Ghana would be free in 1957. (That same year Nkrumah married Fathia Halen Ritzk, with whom he eventually had three children.)

Becomes first president of Ghana republic

On March 6, 1957, Ghana became the first African nation to break free of colonialism. (Almost every African nation south of the Sahara desert at the time was under control of Great Britain, France, Portugal, or other European nations.) Nkrumah was named the first prime minister of the independent republic (his title was changed to president in 1964). He also, at that time, renamed the nation Ghana—after a highly advanced ancient civilization by that name that had flourished in north-central Africa (what is now western Sudan).

Nkrumah did not see Ghana's independence as the final stage of his work. His future tasks included not only strengthening the economic and political institutions of Ghana but also working for the independence of all other colonized African nations. In his autobiography, Nkrumah wrote: "African nationalism was not confined to the Gold Coast—the new Ghana. From now on it must be pan-African nationalism, and the ideology of African political consciousness and African political emancipation must spread throughout the whole continent, into every nook and corner of it."

Nkrumah convened the Organization of African Unity (OAU) in 1958 to address the challenge of creating an independent, united Africa. To underscore Nkrumah's commitment to the pan-Africanist cause, he included a clause in Ghana's constitution of 1960 that the nation would surrender its sovereignty to a Union of African States.

Faces obstacles as leader

As the leader of the first independent African republic, Nkrumah immediately set to work to raise the standard of living of Ghanaians. He instituted social programs such as free health care and education. His literacy program succeeded in making Ghana a nation with one of the highest literacy rates in the continent. He also attempted to modernize Ghana by improving transportation and communication systems. Nkrumah's efforts, however, were hampered by many obstacles.

First, several of Nkrumah's cabinet ministers, who were given great responsibility while Nkrumah traveled on OAU business, were denounced for corruption and mismanagement. In addition, Nkrumah's agricultural policies, which forced farmers to diversify their crops in order to lessen the nation's dependence on the export of cocoa, bred resentment in the countryside. As opposition movements gained strength, Nkrumah cracked down on dissent and imprisoned opposition leaders. There were several assassination attempts against Nkrumah, and rumors spread that the military was planning to take over the government by force.

Deposed in a military coup

On February 24, 1966, the long-anticipated military coup came to pass. Nkrumah was in North Vietnam at the time, attempting to negotiate an end to the Vietnam War (1954–75). The deposed president was immediately offered refuge in Guinea (which achieved its independence from France in 1959), by his friend and political ally Sekou Touré. Touré invited Nkrumah to be honorary copresident of his country (located west of Ghana)—a gesture that recognized Nkrumah's status as the father of African independence.

U.S. Involvement in Nkrumah's Overthrow

There is evidence that the Central Intelligence Agency (CIA)—the international information-gathering arm of the United States government—played a role in the coup that toppled Ghana's leader Kwame Nkrumah. (The administration of President Lyndon B. Johnson [1908–1973]; president 1963–68) was opposed to Nkrumah's growing acceptance of socialism—the form of social organization based on the control of the means of production by the community as a whole, rather than by individuals or corporations.) An early indication of CIA involvement came after the coup, when Khow Amihyia, the principal Ghanaian architect of the military takeover, told reporters that he had been trained by the CIA.

Although CIA interference in Ghanaian affairs had been officially prohibited by a congressional committee and denied by the CIA, former CIA agent John Stockwell revealed in a 1978 book, *In Search of Enemies,* that the CIA station in Accra (the capital of Ghana) funded and otherwise assisted Ghanaian officers involved in the coup. "The Accra (CIA) station was given full, if unofficial credit for the eventual coup," wrote Stockwell. "None of this was adequately reflected in the agency's written records." And a *New York Times* article published in 1978 called the CIA's role in Ghana's 1966 coup "pivotal."

Nkrumah lived out his final years in Guinea, continuing his leadership of the pan-Africanist movement. He wrote two books during that period: *Handbook of Revolutionary Warfare: A Guide to the Armed Phase of African Revolution* (1968) and *Class Struggle in Africa* (1970).

Dies of cancer

Nkrumah was diagnosed with cancer in 1970. He traveled to a hospital in Bucharest, Romania, for treatment the following year, but the disease had progressed too far to be treated. Nkrumah died in Bucharest on April 27, 1972. After lengthy negotiations, the military rulers of Ghana allowed Nkrumah's body to be transported to his home village for burial.

A funeral service for Nkrumah was held in Guinea. Speaking about his friend, President Touré stated: "Nkrumah in his lifetime incarnated the struggle of the African peoples against imperialism, colonialism, and neocolonialism. Nkrumah is not dead and could not die. By paying tribute to his memory the Guinean people are expressing fidelity to the ideals of liberty, democracy and progress, which throughout his life underlay the courageous and untiring activities of our brother, friend, and companion-in-arms, President Kwame Nkrumah."

Sources

Books
Kellner, Douglas. *Kwame Nkrumah*. New York: Chelsea House Publishers, 1987.

McDow, Thomas F. "Nkrumah, Francis Nwia Kofi." *Encyclopedia of Africa South of the Sahara*. Vol. 3. Edited by John Middleton. New York: Charles Scribner's Sons, 1997, pp. 329–30.

Nkrumah, Kwame. *The Autobiography of Kwame Nkrumah*. Edinburgh, Scotland: Thomas Nelson and Sons Ltd., 1957.

Articles
French, Howard W. "A Century Later, Letting Africans Draw Their Own Map." *New York Times*. November 23, 1997: WK5.

Alice Paul

Born January 11, 1885
Moorestown, New Jersey
Died July 9, 1977
Moorestown, New Jersey

Women's rights activist

> "Equality of rights under the law shall not be denied or abridged by the United States or by any State on account of sex."
>
> *Text of the Equal Rights Amendment, authored by Alice Paul in 1923*

Alice Paul introduced the use of militant tactics—such as marches, demonstrations, picketing the White House, and hunger strikes—to the women's suffrage (voting rights) movement. Although her methods landed her and her colleagues in jail, they helped secure the passage of a constitutional amendment guaranteeing women the right to vote. Paul also authored the Equal Rights Amendment (ERA) and campaigned, unsuccessfully, for its adoption for half a century.

Although unquestionably committed to the cause of women's rights, Paul has been criticized for being domineering and elitist and for excluding African American women's rights from her agenda.

A Quaker upbringing

Paul was born in 1885 in Moorestown, New Jersey. She was the oldest of four children in a well-to-do Quaker family. Paul's father, William M. Paul, was a banker and a businessman. Both of Paul's parents instilled in their children traditional Quaker values of social justice, equal rights, and the duty to help oppressed people.

That Paul would become a women's rights activist came as no surprise to her mother, Tacie Parry Paul. In an interview published in the October 1919 issue of *Everybody's Magazine,* Mrs. Paul was asked what she thought of her daughter's political activities. "Well, Mr. Paul always used to say," stated Mrs. Paul, "when there was anything hard and disagreeable to be done, 'I bank on Alice.'"

Extensive education

In her youth Paul was educated by private tutors, after which she went to Swarthmore College in Swarthmore, Pennsylvania. She graduated with a bachelor's degree in 1905, then spent one year studying social work at the New York School of Philanthropy. Her field work at the school involved organizing women workers on New York's Lower East Side. Paul next attended the University of Pennsylvania, where she earned a master's degree in sociology in 1907 and a Ph.D. in 1912. She wrote her dissertation on the legal rights of women.

Paul did much of the course work and research for her Ph.D. in England. She took classes in social work at the University of Birmingham and classes in sociology and economics at the University of London's School of Economics.

Learns radical tactics from British suffragists

Paul's most profound learning experiences in England occurred not in the classroom but in meeting halls and on the streets. Specifically, Paul met women at the fore of the English struggle for woman suffrage. She was taken under the wing of Christabel Pankhurst—one of the most militant British suffragists and a leader of the Women's Social and Political Movement. Paul began attending the group's meetings and demonstrations.

The tactics of the British suffragists were quite radical, especially by the standards of the U.S. women's movement. The Englishwomen forced confrontations with lawmakers and risked arrest. Paul was arrested seven times for participating in demonstrations at the parliament building. During three of her jail stays, Paul refused to eat. Prison authorities responded by force-feeding her through nasal tubes, which is a very painful process.

Lucy Stone

Lucy Stone (1818–1893) was widely regarded as the suffrage movement's best public speaker. Stone, who cut her activist teeth in the movement to end slavery, organized the First National Woman's Rights Convention in 1850. She later cofounded the American Woman Suffrage Association (AWSA) and published the *Women's Journal* (a suffrage newspaper) from 1870 to 1917.

Stone believed in the use of civil disobedience (the refusal to comply with laws one feels are unjust) to further her goal. To that end, in 1858 Stone refused to pay property taxes on the grounds that she was denied the right to vote. She was arrested for this action and her property was auctioned off to pay her taxes.

Stone was also famous for her refusal to take her husband's name after marriage. She argued that in taking a

Lucy Stone. *Courtesy of the Library of Congress.*

husband's name, the woman was giving up her identity. Stone and her husband Harry Blackwell, in contrast to other married couples, defined themselves as "equal partners."

Joins suffrage movement in United States

When Paul returned to the United States in 1912, she brought with her the militancy of the English suffrage movement. She immediately joined the National American Woman Suffrage Association (NAWSA) and took on the responsibility of heading its Congressional Committee. (NAWSA had been formed in 1890 by a merger of the two most prominent suffrage organizations—the National Woman Suffrage Association and the American Woman Suffrage Association.)

Paul's association with NAWSA did not last long. NAWSA members were cautious in their approach to social action and disapproved of the confrontational tactics favored by Paul.

Founds National Woman's Party; pickets White House

In 1913 Paul and Lucy Burns—an American woman she had met while working with the British suffragists—founded a new suffrage organization called the Congressional Union (CU). The CU employed a range of tactics in the push for women's enfranchisement, from lobbying members of Congress to picketing the White House to staging hunger strikes. Their first major event, held on the eve of the presidential inauguration of Woodrow Wilson (1856–1924; president from 1913–21), was a parade of five thousand suffragists through the streets of Washington, D.C.

In 1917 the CU joined with the another suffrage association, the Woman's Party, to form the National Woman's Party (NWP). Beginning that January, the NWP held a nearly constant vigil at the White House gates. They displayed signs calling on President Wilson to demonstrate his commitment to democracy by supporting women's right to vote. The NWP picket drew the ire of many passersby, some of whom shouted insults or even physically assaulted the suffragists.

In October 1917 the suffragists were ordered by the police to leave the White House gate. They refused and were taken to the Occoquan Workhouse jail in Virginia. There Paul began a hunger strike in prison and convinced many of the other detained NWP members to join her. Again, Paul endured painful force-feeding. At the end of November the protesters were released, and two months later Wilson threw his support behind the woman suffrage amendment.

Efforts bear fruit in Nineteenth Amendment

The work of Paul and others in the women's suffrage movement met with success in 1919, when the proposed voting-rights amendment was passed by Congress. Over the next year suffragists successfully campaigned from state to state, until the amendment was ratified by the necessary thirty-six states (ratification by three-fourths of all states is required for the adoption of any Constitutional amendment).

Women in the United States were granted the right to vote in 1920, with the passage of the Nineteenth Amendment. The Nineteenth Amendment reads, in its entirety: "The right of citizens of the United States to vote shall not be denied or abridged by the United States or by any State on account of sex. Congress shall have power to enforce this article by appropriate legislation."

Drafts Equal Rights Amendment

After the victory for woman suffrage, Paul began pushing for women's rights on a broader scale. On behalf of the National Women's Party, Paul drafted an Equal Rights Amendment (ERA). The ERA was to have granted equality to women in all respects of public life. In 1923 the proposed legislation was introduced into Congress but was not approved. For the next six decades, Paul continued her ultimately unsuccessful campaign for the ERA's passage.

Earns law degrees; fights for international women's rights

In 1920 Paul recognized that she would be a more effective advocate for women's rights if she had a thorough understanding of the law. She enrolled in Washington College of Law and in 1922 earned her bachelor of legal letters degree. She continued her studies at American University in Washington, D.C., earning master's and doctoral degrees in law in 1927 and 1928, respectively.

In the 1930s Paul concentrated on international women's rights. She settled in Geneva, Switzerland, and attempted, unsuccessfully, to persuade the Pan American Congress and the League of Nations (the precursor to the United Nations; formed after World War I [1914–18]) to make women's rights part of their platforms. Paul participated in a League of Nations committee on women's issues. In 1938 she founded the World Woman's Party, which later succeeded in getting a commitment to women's rights (including voting rights) included in the charter of the United Nations (formed in 1945 after World War II [1939–45]).

Creates controversy in National Woman's Party

At the outbreak of World War II, Paul returned to Washington, D.C., where she resumed living at the headquarters of the National Woman's Party and working for the passage of the ERA. In the 1940s Congressional support for the ERA mounted. The NWP, however, was weakened by infighting and was not able to effectively advocate for the ERA. Paul was at the center of the controversy. First she was accused of misusing NWP funds. And in the early 1950s several party members quit over Paul's endorsement of Senator Joseph McCarthy's anticommunist crusade. (McCarthy [1909–1957] spearheaded a series of investigations—commonly referred to as "witch-hunts"—from 1950 to 1954 to rid government, educational institutions, and entertainment industries of anyone believed to have communist [antiprivate ownership] leanings.)

Uses civil rights movement to advance women's issues

In the 1950s Paul adopted the strategy of piggybacking women's rights issues onto civil rights issues. Many people criticized Paul for this approach, accusing her of using the burgeoning African American rights movement for her own purposes after previously having ignored the needs of African American women. (During the 1913 march on the eve of Wilson's inauguration, for example, Paul had made African American suffragists march in the back of the procession to avoid offending southern white women.)

Paul was undeterred by the criticism. During congressional debate over the 1964 Civil Rights Act, Paul convinced Howard Smith, a conservative representative from Virginia, to attach a rider to the proposed legislation that would prohibit discrimination in employment based on sex. Smith's action was widely viewed as an attempt to complicate the Civil Rights Act, and thus to hurt the act's chances of succeeding. The act passed, however, and working women have benefitted as a result. (The 1964 Civil Rights Act outlawed discrimination in the areas of education, employment, voting, and public accommodations.)

The defeat of the ERA

In 1972 Paul and other women's rights activists brought a weaker version of the original ERA before Congress.

Congress passed the bill and sent it along to the states for ratification. While two-thirds of the state legislatures approved the amendment, campaigns by conservative organizations prevented its ratification in the other states. To this day, the rights of women are not explicitly defined in the Constitution. (While there are presently numerous laws protecting the rights of women, there is no one piece of sweeping legislation that grants equality to women in all aspects of life.)

The Equal Rights Amendment, as it was proposed in 1972, read:

> *Section 1. Equality of rights under the law shall not be denied by the United States or any state on account of sex.*

> *Section 2. The Congress shall have the power to enforce, by appropriate legislation, the provisions of this article.*

> *Section 3. This amendment shall take effect two years after the date of ratification.*

Final years

In 1972, at the age of eighty-seven, Paul moved to a cottage in Ridgefield, Connecticut, and continued her work by telephone. In 1974 she suffered a stroke, after which she moved into a Quaker nursing home in her hometown of Moorestown, New Jersey.

In 1977, as Paul's ninety-second birthday neared, ERA ratification still stood four states away. The National Organization for Women (NOW) used the occasion of Paul's birthday to renew the push for ratification. NOW members visited legislators in states that had not voted for ratification, urging them to deliver their support for the ERA as a birthday present for Paul. Paul died later that year, and the ERA was never ratified.

Sources

Books

"Paul, Alice." *American National Biography.* Edited by John A. Garraty and Mark C. Carnes. New York: Oxford University Press, 1999, pp. 156–58.

Irwin, Inez Haynes. *The Story of the Woman's Party.* New York: Harcourt, Brace and Company, 1921.

Levinson, Nancy Smiler. *The First Women Who Spoke Out.* Minneapolis: Dillon Press, Inc., 1983.

McGuire, William, and Leslie Wheeler. *American Social Leaders.* Santa Barbara, CA: ABC-CLIO, 1993, pp. 361–62.

Stevens, Doris. *Jailed for Freedom: American Women Win the Vote.* Troutdale, OR: NewSage Press, 1995.

Wheeler, Marjorie Spruill, ed. *One Woman, One Vote: Rediscovering the Woman Suffrage Movement.* Troutdale, OR: NewSage Press, 1995.

Articles

Olson, Tod. "One Person, One Vote." *Scholastic Update.* October 7, 1994: 15+.

Wedemeyer, Dee. "A Salute to the E.R.A. Originator." *New York Times.* January 10, 1977.

Web Sites

"Alice Paul." National Women's Hall of Fame. [Online] Available http://www.greatwomen.org/paul/htm (accessed February 11, 2000).

Margaret Randall

Born December 6, 1936
New York, New York

Author, poet, feminist activist, and teacher

Margaret Randall, who describes herself as "a leftist, a feminist, a teacher, a writer, a mother," has worked to support the revolutionary societies of Cuba and Nicaragua and has written and edited more than fifty books of prose and poetry.

Margaret Randall.
Photograph by Peter Kelly.
Reproduced by permission of Impact Visuals.

Margaret Randall made headlines in 1985 when she was ordered to leave the United States under a McCarthy-era statute called the McCarran-Walter Act. The Immigration and Naturalization Service claimed that Randall had renounced her U.S. citizenship by accepting Mexican citizenship in the 1960s. The agency sought to deport Randall because her writings were deemed to "advocate the economic, international and governmental doctrines of world communism." In 1989 Randall's U.S. citizenship was restored by the Immigration Appeals Board, and the motion to deport her was dismissed.

Grows up in New York and New Mexico

Randall was born to an upper-middle-class family in New York City on December 6, 1936. Her parents were world travelers with a penchant for unconventional and countercultural people and places. When Randall was in sixth grade, her family moved to New Mexico.

After high school she attended the University of New Mexico, in Albuquerque, for one year. In 1955 she married Sam

Jacobs, a semiprofessional hockey player, and dropped out of school to pay for her husband's education. The couple lived in Spain for one year; their marriage ended in divorce in 1958.

Joins the Beat movement

In the fall of 1958 Randall moved back to New York, home of the burgeoning Beat movement. (The Beat movement was comprised of young poets, artists, writers, and others who rejected what they saw as the rigid conformity and materialism of mainstream American culture. Among the most famous Beats were poet Allen Ginsberg [1926–1997; author of *Howl*] and writer Jack Kerouac [1922–1969; author of *On the Road*].) Randall settled on the Lower East Side where rent and food was inexpensive. Like many of her friends in the Beat movement, she worked in a series of part-time, low-paying jobs and spent most of her time pursuing her real passion: writing. She frequented coffee houses and bars where poetry was read and political ideas were debated.

Edits political journal in Mexico City

In 1961, tired of the New York Beat scene, Randall (with her infant son, who had been fathered by a New York poet) moved to Mexico City, Mexico. At that time the Mexican capital was home to a large community of poets and political dissidents from the United States and Latin America. Soon after her arrival Randall met poet Sergio Mondragon, and the two were wed. They began a literary journal called *El Corno Emplumado* (The Plumed Horn) in which they published poetry and radical political writings.

The couple produced their journal for eight years, during which time Randall gave birth to two more children. The responsibility for day-to-day operations of the journal fell increasingly to Randall, as Mondragon devoted more and more of his time to meditation and poetry. In 1966 Randall was forced to find extra work in order to support her family. To facilitate finding employment, Randall applied for and received Mexican citizenship.

The year 1968 saw an explosion of student protests in many parts of the world, including Mexico City. When students took over the campus of the national university in Mex-

Randall Speaks About Cuban Women

After returning to the United States, Randall lectured widely on the status of women in Cuba and Nicaragua. The following passage about Cuban women is from a talk given at the University of Michigan in 1986.

"Cuba, before the victory of the (1959) revolution, was not much more than a sort of house of pleasure for U.S. businessmen and U.S. marines. There was a nightclub in Havana called the Tropicana with its own private airstrip—U.S. magnates came down and used that nightclub and the people in it, essentially the women in it and the women on the streets of Havana and . . . other cities, pretty much at their whim and will. . . . "

"When the Cuban movement came to victory in 1959, it was a liberating force for women. . . . Education was opened up to women in a vast sort of way. It didn't take more than four or five years for large numbers of women to begin to go into some of the areas that had previously been almost off-limits to them, such as engineering, architecture, and medicine. The percentages of women in those fields rose very quickly: six to seven years after the revolution some 50 percent of the graduating physicians were women, so in that area the movement was very swift.

"The Family Code came out of [a government-sponsored commission on the status of women]. The Family Code is a whole package of legislation regarding family life, family obligations, the obligations of men and women to their children, children to their parents and so forth. The foremost clauses . . . which are included in the marriage contract and read into the marriage ceremonies as well, cover the obligation that a man has to do 50 percent of the household work, 50 percent of childcare, and in fact, support his wife in making her situation equal to his in terms of a chance to study, a chance to better her professional education, a chance to make of her life what she as an individual wishes to make of it, instead of being trapped in a domestic situation which somehow never permits this."

ico City, soldiers responded by opening fire. Hundreds of students were killed, and leftists (people who favored extensive social reform hoping that it would result in greater personal freedoms and improved social conditions) were hunted throughout the city. Fearing for their lives, Randall and her children fled to Cuba. By that time Randall and Mondragon had divorced.

Works in Cuba and Nicaragua

Randall's choice of Cuba as her haven was a political one: Cuban rebels had toppled the U.S.-backed dictator Fulgencio Batista (1901–1973) in 1959 and had established a socialist government. (Socialism is a social and economic system based on the control of the means of production by the community as a whole, rather than by wealthy individuals or corporations.) The Cuban government, led by President Fidel Castro (see box in **"Ché" Guevara** entry) sought to improve the standard of living for Cuba's poorest citizens by redistributing land and nationalizing (taking government control of) the island's natural resources and industries. Castro and his policies were (and still are) strongly opposed by the U.S. government

Randall was hired as an editor at a Cuban government-run publishing company. She worked there until 1975, then for the next five years made her living as a freelance writer and photographer. While in Cuba Randall published several works, including collections of poems, observations on life in socialist Cuba, and feminist studies.

In 1980 Randall moved to Nicaragua—a small Central American country, the people of which had the previous year overthrown U.S.-backed dictator Anastasio Somoza (1925–1980). Randall first worked as a publicist for the Nicaraguan Ministry of Culture and then as a staff member of the Foreign Press Center. During her four years in Nicaragua, Randall wrote extensively about the country and the changes the revolution had brought. She especially focused on the gains made by Nicaraguan women in the revolutionary society and the role of "liberation theology" (a religious movement that seeks to improve conditions for poor people) in bringing about revolutionary change.

Returns home and faces deportation proceedings

In 1984, after twenty-three years of living in Latin America, Randall decided to return to the United States to be near her aging parents and to teach at the University of New Mexico. She moved to Albuquerque, New Mexico, with one of her daughters and her American husband, Floyce Alexander. Soon after settling in, she was ordered by the Immigration and

McCarran-Walter Act Keeps "Undesirables" at Bay

The 1952 McCarran-Walter Act, passed during the height of anti-communist hysteria in the United States, guarantees the U.S. government the right to exclude or deport any alien who might "engage in activities which would be prejudicial to the public interest, or endanger the welfare, safety or security of the United States." The act also provides for the exclusion of any person who may advocate or engage in terrorist, Communist, or subversive activities.

Since its passage, the McCarran-Walter Act has been used to keep more than forty thousand people out of the United States, including such notables as Chilean poet Pablo Neruda, Mexican novelist Carlos Fuentes, English novelist Graham Greene, Canadian writer Farley Mowat, Colombian novelist Gabriel García Márquez, and Colombian journalist Patricia Lara. In a very high-profile case, the Act also prevented Hortensia de Allende, the widow of slain Chilean socialist president **Salvador Allende** (see entry) from visiting the United States from 1983 to 1987.

In January 1986 the McCarran-Walter Act was used as the basis for the arrests of seven Palestinian men and the Kenyan wife of one of the men, in the Los Angeles, California, area. The eight immigrants were held in isolation at the Terminal Island prison for ten days and threatened with deportation. Their crime was distributing pro-Palestinian literature.

The INS accused the eight of "fostering the actions of a terrorist group" (the Palestine Liberation Organization) and advocating "world communism." Lawyers for the "L.A. Eight," as the group was called, claimed that their clients were arrested for an activity that is protected by the First Amendment and convinced a district court judge to issue an injunction stopping the deportations. Government lawyers argued that First Amendment rights do not extend to noncitizens. The government's position was rejected by numerous courts. The government has not yet appealed the case to the Supreme Court, but the threat of deportation still lingers over the L.A. Eight.

Naturalization Service (INS) to leave the country. She had been deemed an undesirable alien.

Randall was informed that by taking on Mexican citizenship in 1966, she had given up her U.S. citizenship. Randall responded that she had not renounced or overridden her U.S. citizenship when taking on Mexican citizenship. The reason she took out Mexican citizenship, she explained, was to make it easier for her to find employment.

Targeted because of alleged communist beliefs

The INS brought deportation charges against Randall under a little-known subsection of the Immigration and Nationality Act, called the McCarran-Walter Act. The McCarran-Walter Act provides for the exclusion from the country of any alien deemed undesirable (for a great number of reasons) by the U.S. government (see box). In the deportation order, the INS stated that Randall's writings went "far beyond mere dissent, disagreement with, or criticism of the U.S. or its policies . . . [and] advocate[d] the economic, international and governmental doctrines of world communism."

Randall referred to her case as an assault on First Amendment rights. That claim was bolstered by the nature of her deportation hearing, where the content of her writings was placed in the spotlight. One of the questions posed to Randall at the hearing was, "How did you feel about publishing a magazine that also published communists?" According to Randall, "The [government] had pages and pages of my books, magazine articles, and poems. I had written a poem to **"Ché" Guevara** (1928–1967; see entry) when he died. That proved I was a 'communist.'"

Randall won her case in 1989 when an Immigration Appeals Board decided that she was, in fact, a dual citizen of the United States and Mexico. As a U.S. citizen, she could not be deported.

Recent years of writing and teaching

Since returning to the United States, Randall has authored numerous books and articles. She has also lectured widely on college campuses throughout the nation. Randall divorced her third husband, Floyce Alexander, in 1984. Since 1986 she has lived with a female partner, Barbara Byers.

In 1986 Randall published *Albuquerque, Coming Back to the U.S.A.,* and in 1992 *Dancing with the Doe: New and Selected Poems, 1986–1991.* Her 1994 book, *Sandino's Daughters Revisited: Feminism in Nicaragua,* explores Nicaraguan feminism after the demise of the Sandinista revolution (led by **Augusto Sandino** [see entry] against Nicaraguan dictator Somoza) through interviews with twelve prominent Nicaraguan women. And in 1997 Randall examined the role of money in the family and in society with the publication of *The Price You Pay: The Hidden Cost of Women's Relationship to Money.*

Randall has held a number of teaching positions since the mid-1980s at institutions including the University of New Mexico; Trinity College in Hartford, Connecticut; Oberlin College in Ohio; Macalester College in St. Paul, Minnesota; and the University of Delaware. She served as managing editor of *Frontiers: A Journal of Women Studies* in the early 1990s.

Sources

Books
"Margaret Randall." *Contemporary Poets.* 6th ed. Detroit: St. James Press, 1996.

Randall, Margaret. *Christians in the Nicaraguan Revolution.* Vancouver Canada: New Star Books, 1981.

Randall, Margaret. *Part of the Solution: Portrait of a Revolutionary.* New York: New Directions Publishing, 1973.

Randall, Margaret. *Sandino's Daughters: Testimonies of Nicaraguan Women in Struggle.* Vancouver, Canada: New Star Books, 1981.

Articles
Engelbert, Phillis. "Limiting Debate: McCarthyism in the 80s." *AGENDA.* May 1987: 2+.

Fetherling, Douglas. "Reciprocity in Exiles." *Canadian Business and Current Affairs.* April 1997: 39–40.

Martinez, Demetria. "Book Deals with Secrets, Lies, Silence about Money." *National Catholic Reporter.* November 14, 1997: 20.

Randall, Margaret. "Cuban and Nicaraguan Women." *AGENDA.* May, 1986: 1+.

Randall, Margaret. "Words That Express Our Realities Deserve to be Praised, Preserved." *National Catholic Reporter.* June 28, 1996: 21+.

"Sandino's Daughters Revisited: Feminism in Nicaragua." *Publishers Weekly.* January 31, 1994: 83.

Web Sites
Margaret Randall. [Online] Available http://hrcr.law.columbia.edu/ccr/randall.html (accessed February 29, 2000).

A. Philip Randolph

Born April 15, 1889
Crescent City, Florida
Died May 16, 1979
New York, New York

Labor leader and civil rights activist

As founding president, A. Philip Randolph led the Brotherhood of Sleeping Car Porters to become the first successful black labor union in the United States. Randolph was instrumental in forcing the integration of the U.S. armed forces and for securing equal rights for African Americans in the workplace. He was the national director of the historic 1963 March on Washington for Peace, Jobs, and Justice.

Humble beginnings

Asa Philip Randolph was born in 1889 in Crescent City, Florida, into a poor family. Randolph's father, James William Randolph, was a minister and a tailor. His mother, Elizabeth Robinson Randolph, had given birth to her first son, James, Jr., when she was just fifteen years old. She had Asa two years later. Despite the family's difficulties making ends meet, James William Randolph tutored his sons in reading and refused to use segregated facilities. (Randolph grew up during the Jim Crow era, from the 1890s through the 1960s, in which the separation of races on every level of society was mandated by laws and social customs.)

"This civil rights revolution is not confined to the Negro, nor is it confined to civil rights, for our white allies know that they cannot be free while we are not, and we know that we have no future in a society in which six million white and black people are unemployed and millions live in poverty."

Asa Philip Randolph, 1963

A. Philip Randolph.
Reproduced by permission of AP/Wide World photos.

Randolph did well in school. His grades were excellent and he showed great talent in singing, acting, and sports. He was named class valedictorian at his all-African American high school and graduated in 1907.

Undergoes political awakening in New York City

In 1911 Randolph headed for New York City, where he hoped to find work as an actor. Instead, he worked at a series of menial jobs. A year after arriving in the city Randolph took advantage of the free education offered by the City College of New York. There he came in contact with student activists, particularly those involved in the socialist cause. (Socialism is a type of social and economic organization based on the control of the means of production by the community as a whole, rather than by wealthy individuals or corporations.) Randolph formed a discussion and action group called the Independent Political Council, where he debated ideas with other students.

Randolph married a beauty salon operator named Lucille Campbell Green in 1914. Green was fun-loving and outgoing, in contrast to the formal and reserved Randolph. The two formed a life-long partnership. They never had children.

Edits the *Messenger*

In 1917 Randolph joined forces with his friend, socialist activist Chandler Owen, and started a magazine called the *Messenger.* The publication, which remained in print through 1928, focused on politics and black culture. At its peak, in 1919, the *Messenger* had a circulation of 26,000. Randolph used the byline "A. Philip Randolph"—the name by which he became known for the rest of his life.

Randolph and Owen, in the pages of the *Messenger,* were sharply critical of U.S. participation in World War I (1914–18). The pair were arrested for their views in 1918, only to be released by a judge who did not believe that they, as African Americans, could be intelligent enough to have authored the articles.

Organizes Brotherhood of Sleeping Car Porters

In 1925 Randolph was asked by a Pullman porter named Ashley L. Totten to help him form a porters' union. The Pullman porters were African American men, mostly well-educated, who worked on the passenger trains of the Pullman Rail Car Company. Although a porter's wages were low (the bulk of a porter's earnings were from tips) and the hours were long, the job was considered one of the most prestigious available to African Americans at the time.

The Brotherhood of Sleeping Car Porters (BSCP) was founded at a mass meeting of porters on August 25, 1925. Randolph and the union members, however, faced a long and bitter struggle with the Pullman Company for recognition. The company tried to break the union by harassing and firing activists and by refusing to enter into negotiations. Due to the perseverance of the union members and Randolph's capable and charismatic leadership, the BSCP prevailed. In the summer of 1935 the BSCP became the nation's first legally recognized African American labor union. Pullman was forced to negotiate a contract that included higher wages and improved working conditions for the porters.

Many historians consider the BSCP's victory to have laid the groundwork for the civil rights movement of the 1950s and 1960s.

Presses for equal treatment of African American workers in wartime

Randolph used his considerable influence to end discrimination against African American workers in defense-related industries during World War II (1939–45). In 1939, when the war began in Europe, the U.S. War Department (later renamed the Defense Department) made the decision to stockpile arms in case the United States was to enter the conflict. Thousands of southern African Americans headed north in search of the well-paying jobs in defense plants. When they reached their destinations, however, they were either refused jobs or offered low-paying segregated positions.

To protest the unfair working conditions for African Americans, Randolph called for a national march to be held in the summer of 1941. He predicted he could attract one hundred thousand African American workers to demonstrate in Washington, D.C.

President Franklin D. Roosevelt (1882–1945; president from 1933–45) scrambled to head off the protest action. He knew that such a march would be divisive, and he wished to keep the country united behind the war effort. Just six days before the planned march Roosevelt acquiesced. On June 25, 1941, he signed a presidential order prohibiting job discrimination in defense-related industries with government contracts.

Forces desegregation of the military

Although victorious in the worker-discrimination matter, Randolph had not met with similar success in his attempt to convince Roosevelt to desegregate the military. In the armed forces, black troops were assigned to separate lower-paying units, were given menial jobs such as working in the kitchen or digging trenches, and were rarely promoted to the rank of officer.

Upon Roosevelt's death in 1945, Randolph met with Roosevelt's successor, Harry Truman (1884–1972; president from 1945–53). Randolph told Truman that if he did not order the desegregation of the armed forces, lower-payings would no longer serve. Randolph also testified before the U.S. Senate. He claimed that unless equality prevailed, African Americans would "refuse to fight as slaves for a democracy they cannot possess and enjoy." After a long and bitter debate among members of Congress, Truman, in 1948, signed an executive order guaranteeing equal treatment to all members of the military regardless of race.

Works with AFL-CIO and Negro American Labor Council

In 1955 the nation's two largest labor unions, the American Federation of Labor (AFL) and the Congress of Industrial Organizations (CIO), united, and Randolph was one of two African Americans named to the AFL-CIO executive committee. Four years later, after a series of confrontations with the AFL-CIO president George Meany, Randolph resigned.

Randolph then established a separate organization for African American workers, called the Negro American Labor Council (NALC). The purpose of the NALC was to publicize racial discrimination in the mainstream labor unions. He remained at the helm of that group until 1964.

Renews proposal for March on Washington

In the spring of 1963 Randolph resurrected the idea of the national march he had proposed eighteen years earlier. The "March for Jobs and Freedom," as Randolph called it, demanded desegregation of public facilities, an end to discrimination in employment, decent housing and education, and the right of African Americans to vote.

The timing of the proposed march coincided with President John F. Kennedy's (1917–1963; president from 1961–63) introduction of a sweeping civil rights bill that would outlaw segregation of all public accommodations, speed up school desegregation, and make it easier for African Americans to register to vote. Leaders of every major civil rights organization saw Randolph's march as a way of showing support for the proposed legislation. In order to reflect the broader agenda, the event was renamed the "March on Washington for Peace, Jobs, and Justice."

The March on Washington

On the morning of Wednesday, August 28, 1963, 250,000 people (among them 60,000 whites) descended upon Washington, D.C., in the largest protest march to that date. People from all walks of life—teachers, students, union members, church groups, and unemployed people—arrived on approximately two thousand chartered buses and thirty trains, in cars, and on foot. A group of Hollywood celebrities flew in on chartered planes. The day had the feel of a celebration or, in the words of Ralph Abernathy (1926–1996; former leader of the Southern Christian Leadership Conference [SCLC]), "a jubilation."

The significance of the March on Washington is underscored in the book *Eyes on the Prize* by Juan Williams. " . . . America witnessed an unprecedented spectacle that day," wrote Williams. "The march brought joy and a sense of possibility to people throughout the nation who perhaps had not understood the civil rights movement before or who had felt threatened by it."

Overcomes Kennedy's objections

President Kennedy, as it turned out, disapproved of the planned march. On June 22, 1963, Kennedy called together

Bayard Rustin

Bayard Rustin (1912–1987) was A. Philip Randolph's right-hand man in the planning of national marches in both 1941 and 1963. Rustin's involvement in the civil rights movement and the international movement for freedom and human rights spanned fifty years. From Montgomery, Alabama, to Washington, D.C., to Delhi, India, Rustin worked behind the scenes to bring about social change. He composed and sang freedom songs, wrote pamphlets, placed his body on the line to challenge segregation (the forced, legal separation of the races), raised money, recruited people to the cause, and taught organizing tactics to civil rights leaders. Rustin's crowning achievement was his coordination of the 1963 March on Washington for Peace, Jobs, and Justice.

Rustin was born in West Chester, Pennsylvania, on March 17, 1912, to a family of pacifists and Quakers (a religious organization that stresses nonviolence and simple living). His involvement in social causes began at an early age, with his membership in the Young Communist League in Harlem, New York.

A lifelong pacifist, Rustin refused induction into the army during World War II (1939–45). As a result, he spent twenty-eight months in prison. There he met other radical pacifists, some of whom later founded the Congress on Racial Equality (CORE). After his release from prison in 1945, Rustin worked with the pacifist antiracist group Fellowship of Reconciliation to organize the Journey of Reconciliation (JOR). The JOR was a bus ride through the segregated American South by integrated groups of people—it was the late 1940s precursor to the 1961 Freedom Rides.

Rustin also headed the Free India Committee in the United States in the late 1940s, leading demonstrations in front of the British embassy in support of India's independence from the colonial power. Rustin traveled to India and Africa in the early 1950s, where he met with the sons of slain Indian independence leader

thirty civil rights leaders for a meeting at the White House and tried to talk them out of staging the event. He said that he felt the march would hurt the chances of passage of his civil rights bill; he also feared that the demonstration could turn violent.

Randolph, considered by that time the elder statesman of the civil rights movement, responded by reminding Kennedy that African Americans were already holding civil

Bayard Rustin. *Reproduced by permission of AP/Wide World Photos.*

Mohandas Gandhi (1869–1948; see entry) and studied nonviolence. He also supported **Kwame Nkrumah** (1909–1972; see entry) in his bid to make Ghana the first independent African country. In 1957, near the start of the Montgomery bus boycott, Rustin mentored **Martin Luther King, Jr.,** (1929–1968; see entry) in the tenets of Gandhian nonviolence.

Regardless of his organizational genius and unwavering commitment to social justice, Rustin was never fully accepted by leaders in the civil rights movement, largely because of his prior affiliation with communists and because he was gay. In his early years Rustin had tried to conceal his homosexuality. In the late 1960s and early 1970s, however, he acknowledged his homosexuality and spoke out in favor of gay rights.

From 1965 until the early 1970s, Rustin served as executive director of the New York City-based civil rights organization the A. Philip Randolph Institute (APRI). The APRI's mission included safeguarding the rights of black workers, sponsoring voter registration drives, supporting political candidates, and advising civil rights leaders. The organization continues to fight for racial equality and economic justice. In the 1970s and 1980s, while remaining honorary president of the APRI, Rustin traveled widely in the United States and abroad, giving lectures and educating people about civil and human rights.

rights demonstrations all across America. "If they are bound to be in the streets in any case," said Randolph, "is it not better that they be led by organizations dedicated to civil rights and disciplined by struggle rather than to leave them to other leaders who care neither about civil rights nor about nonviolence?"

The march went ahead, with the reluctant endorsement of Kennedy. It was directed by the leaders of the "big six" civil rights organizations—in addition to Randolph (the march's national director), representing the Negro American Labor Council, the leadership consisted of **Martin Luther King, Jr.**, (see entry) of the Southern Christian Leadership Conference, John Lewis of the **Student Nonviolent Coordinating Committee** (see entry), Roy Wilkins of the National Association for the Advancement of Colored People, James Farmer of the Congress on Racial Equality, and Whitney Young of the National Urban League.

The march, which was the largest in the nation's capital to that date, went ahead without incident. Kennedy was never able to see his bill passed; he was assassinated on November 22, 1963. The bill was signed into law on July 2, 1964, as the 1964 Civil Rights Act, by Kennedy's successor, President Lyndon B. Johnson (1908–1973; president from 1963–69).

Final years

Randolph in his later years was often referred to as the "father of the civil rights movement." In 1971 he was granted an honorary degree from Harvard University, in Cambridge, Massachusetts. Randolph lived his final years in Harlem, in New York City, where his health consistently deteriorated. He died on May 16, 1979, at the age of ninety.

In 1989 the U.S. Postal Service celebrated Black History Month by issuing a stamp bearing Randolph's likeness. And the A. Philip Randolph/Pullman Porter Museum Gallery, on S. Maryland St. in Chicago, Illinois, was established in 1989 to pay tribute to his life and work.

Sources

Books

Anderson, Jervis. *A Philip Randolph: A Biographical Portrait.* New York: Harcourt Brace Jovanovich, Inc., 1972.

Bolden, Tanya. *Strong Men Keep Coming: The Book of African American Men.* New York: John Wiley & Sons, Inc., 1999.

Hanley, Sally. *A. Philip Randolph: Labor Leader.* New York: Chelsea House Publishers, 1989.

Levine, Michael L. *African Americans and Civil Rights From 1619 to the Present.* Phoenix, AZ: Oryx Press, 1996.

McGuire, William, and Leslie Wheeler. *American Social Leaders*. Santa Barbara, CA: ABC-CLIO, 1993, pp. 318–83.

Pfeffer, Paula F. *A. Philip Randolph, Pioneer of the Civil Rights Movement*. Baton Rouge: Louisiana State University Press, 1990.

Williams, Juan. *Eyes on the Prize: America's Civil Rights Years, 1954–1965*. New York: Penguin Books, 1987.

Web Sites

A. Philip Randolph/Pullman Porter Museum Gallery. [Online] Available http://www.wimall.com/pullportermu/ (accessed February 16, 2000).

John Reed

Born October 20, 1887
Portland, Oregon
Died October 17, 1920
Moscow, Russia

Journalist and revolutionary political activist

"We, who are Socialists, must hope . . . that out of the horror of destruction will come far-reaching social changes. This is not our war."

John Reed, "The Traders' War," published in The Masses, *September 1914*

John Reed was an adventurous, revolutionary journalist whose enthusiasm for reporting on world events was matched by his zeal for participating in those events. Reed came of age in New York City's Greenwich Village in the early twentieth century, then a hotbed of political radicalism. With no shortage of left-leaning (favoring extensive social reform with the goal of creating greater personal freedoms and improved social conditions) publications to write for, Reed was sent to cover worker strikes, the Mexican Revolution (1910–20), and World War I (1914–18). Reed spent the final years of his life supporting the Soviet Revolution and advocating a communist movement in the United States. (Communism is the theory of social organization based on the holding of all property in common.)

Wealthy upbringing and education

John Silas Reed was born on October 20, 1887, in Portland, Oregon. His father, Charles Jerome Reed, was a successful businessman, and his mother, Margaret Green, was a descendant of wealthy pioneers. Reed was a sickly child, beset with a long-term kidney ailment. He was educated at home until the age of twelve, during which time his brother Harry was his only playmate. Reed became an avid reader and attended high school at the Portland Academy. He then went to a college preparatory school called Morristown, in New Jersey.

In 1906 Reed enrolled in Harvard University in Cambridge, Massachusetts. There he sharpened his writing skills and became a campus leader. He wrote for student publications, acted in plays, and participated in sports. Reed graduated in 1910, intent on becoming a journalist.

Establishes career as a writer

After graduation Reed traveled to Europe, hoping to learn more about the world. He earned his fare by working on a freight ship, then spent several months touring England and France.

Upon his return to the United States, Reed headed for New York City's Greenwich Village—home to artists, poets, writers, and social activists. There Reed met and formed a friendship with anarchist and workers-rights-advocate **Emma Goldman** (1869–1940; see entry). (An anarchist is one opposed to all organized forms of government.) Reed also met journalist Lincoln Steffens (1866–1936), a friend of his father's, who helped Reed gain employment at a popular magazine called *American.* At the same time Reed sold news articles and essays to other magazines, including *Collier's* and *Trend.*

In November 1911 *American* rejected a news feature Reed had written about the Harvard University administration's attempt to snuff out activism on campus. The reason for the rejection, Reed discovered, was that the *American* did not want to create controversy. Thus he learned an important lesson about the media's self-imposed limits on its own freedoms.

Edits *The Masses*

At the end of 1912 Reed was invited to join the editorial staff of *The Masses,* a political and literary journal that claimed to publish "free and spirited expressions of every kind." Reed developed a close working relationship with the journal's founder Max Eastman (1883–1969). Reed and Eastman, in the years to come, would be brought up on charges of treason for their magazine's increasingly antiestablishment stance.

In the spring of 1913 Reed traveled to Paterson, New Jersey, to report on a strike by twenty-five thousand silk workers. The workers were demanding an eight-hour workday. Their action was met with arrests and beatings by law enforcement officials. Reed himself was arrested (the first time of many) for scuffling with a police officer. He was held for four days and then released.

Reports on Mexican Revolution

In late 1913 Reed received assignments from *New York World* and *Metropolitan Magazine* to cover the revolution underway in Mexico (see box). Reed interviewed rebel leader Pancho Villa (1877–1923) at his headquarters in Chihuahua, Mexico, then headed south to the scene of the fighting. There he witnessed the massacre of a group of peasant rebel fighters by government forces and wrote about the event. Reed reportedly joined the struggle and was made a staff officer by Villa. Through his journal articles, plus his 1914 book about his experiences in Mexico called *Insurgent Mexico,* Reed provided the American public with a greater understanding of the political forces at work in Mexico. At the same time he gained for himself a measure of fame.

Covers coal miner massacre

In the spring of 1914 Reed headed off on his next journalistic adventure—to the coal miner strike in Ludlow, Colorado. Reed reported on the massacre of twenty-six miners by security guards. The guards, after killing the miners with machine guns, had set fire to the miners' homes. Reed's articles about the strike were sharply critical of businessman and philanthropist John D. Rockefeller (1839–1937), whose holdings included the Ludlow mine.

Travels to Europe during World War I

In August 1914, with the outbreak of World War I in Europe, *Metropolitan* magazine sent Reed abroad to report on the fighting. Reed traveled to France and unsuccessfully tried

The Mexican Revolution

The Mexican Revolution (1910–20) was a bloody struggle to end thirty years of authoritarian rule. Under dictator Porfirio Díaz (1830–1915), a tiny proportion of Mexicans had controlled a tremendous amount of wealth while the majority of the population had lived in poverty. In 1910 forces opposed to that system began to wage war against the government. Rebels pushed for the redistribution of farmland to landless peasants and other social reforms.

While there were several factions fighting for control of the country, the two main revolutionary leaders were Pancho Villa (1877–1923) and **Emiliano Zapata** (1879–1919; see entry). Villa raised a ragged rebel army in the north and began invading army strongholds. Meanwhile, Zapata gathered a mostly indigenous force in the south and took on the political strongmen and their security forces in the countryside. The war officially ended in 1920. Most of the reforms sought by Villa, Zapata, and other leaders, however, were not implemented until 1934, when Lázaro Cárdenas took over as president.

to reach the front. As he learned more about the financial concerns at the root of the war (specifically the desire of European powers to expand their markets and potential profits), as well as the bloody slaughters occurring on the battlefields, his opposition to the war grew. In an article titled "The Traders' War," published in *The Masses* in September 1914, Reed wrote, "We, who are Socialists, must hope . . . that out of the horror of destruction will come far-reaching social changes." Addressing his fellow Americans, Reed wrote, "This is not our war."

After a brief respite in the United States, Reed returned to Europe in March 1915. That time he attempted to reach the front lines through Greece, Serbia, and Russia. In 1916 Reed published a book recounting his wartime experiences, called *The War in Western Europe.* That November he married a journalist from Portland, Oregon, named Louise Bryant.

Reed vigorously opposed the United States government's decision to enter World War I in April 1917. Testifying before the Congressional Committee on Military Affairs, Reed stated: "I do not believe in this war [and] I would not serve in it." Reed, if drafted, would have received a medical waiver from military service because he had a kidney removed in 1916.

Reed's antiwar stance cost him his employment with the *Metropolitan*. But he kept writing for the *New York Mail* and *The Masses*. *The Masses* took an especially strong stand against United States involvement in the war. In 1918 the paper was shut down under the 1917 Espionage Act, and Eastman was brought to trial for treason (the trial resulted in a hung jury—meaning the jury split on its opinion and failed to return a conviction). Eastman later began a new publication that was less strident than *The Masses,* called *The Liberator.*

Participates in Russian revolution

While in Europe, Reed had closely followed events in Russia. In March 1917 the revolutionary struggle against the czar (absolute ruler) had begun. That August Reed and Bryant set sail for Russia to report on and participate in the historic happenings. The couple enthusiastically supported the Bolsheviks, a revolutionary socialist group headed by Vladimir Lenin (1870–1924). The Bolsheviks advocated worldwide socialism and intended to make Russia a nation run by and for workers. (Socialism is a type of social and economic organization based on the control of the means of production by the community as a whole, rather than by wealthy individuals or corporations).

Reed and Bryant arrived in Russia just in time to witness the final stages of the Bolshevik revolution. Reed interviewed several revolutionary leaders, including Leon Trotsky (1879–1940)—an intellectual leader and Lenin's right-hand man. Reed then offered his services as a writer and began producing pamphlets about the revolution for international distribution. Reed met Lenin in January 1918, and the two became close friends. Lenin convinced Reed to address the Soviet Congress on behalf of Americans supportive of the Bolshevik cause.

Arrested for sedition

Reed's troubles with the U.S. government began in the spring of 1918, when he returned to the United States. He was arrested and charged with conspiracy to obstruct the draft (for encouraging American youth not to fight in World War I). His papers—primarily notes of his experiences in Europe and Russia—were seized. Reed's trial ended in a hung jury.

Reed next went on a lecture tour of the United States, rallying support for the revolution in Russia and for worldwide socialism. Reed's fiery speeches led to his arrest in three cities on charges of sedition (treason) and inciting to riot. In none of the cases was Reed convicted.

In November 1918 Reed's papers were returned, and he began writing his famous eyewitness account of the Russian revolution, *Ten Days that Shook the World*. The book was published in March 1919. It won critical acclaim and was characterized as the finest eyewitness account of the Russian revolution (although some criticized it as being biased in favor of the Bolsheviks). Later that year Reed issued a second edition of the book, which included an introduction by Lenin.

Helps form Communist Labor Party

Reed next took on the task of strengthening the communist movement in the United States. To that end he joined the Socialist Party and begin editing the *New York Communist*.

In August 1919, following his expulsion from the Socialist Party (which did not share Reed's enthusiasm for the Bolsheviks), Reed cofounded the Communist Labor Party. He maintained communications between his communist party and the Communist International (Comintern) organization in the Soviet Union. He also edited the party's newspaper, *Voice of Labor*. In that period Reed became increasingly attracted to the philosophy of the Industrial Workers of the World (IWW). The IWW was a burgeoning radical labor organization that sought to form one big union of all the world's workers (see entry on **Joe Hill**).

That summer Reed was once again charged with sedition. Before he was to stand trial, however, he obtained a false passport and left the United States.

Returns to Soviet Union

Reed returned to the Soviet Union in September 1919, seeking aid and direction for the growing American communist movement. Reed, however, was dismayed at the extent of famine and disease he witnessed in the Soviet Union. He also found himself at odds with Lenin's increasing hold on power (Reed favored a democratic decision-making process).

In February 1920, laden with jewels and money the Comintern had given him to assist the American communist movement, Reed headed back to the United States. He traveled via Finland, where he was arrested and charged with smuggling. After being imprisoned for four months, Reed was released in June 1920. He was in poor health and feared a trial for treason in the United States, causing him to return to the Soviet Union.

Reed's wife traveled to meet him that September, but his health continued to decline. Reed died of typhus in Moscow, in the Soviet Union, on October 17, 1920. He was buried on the grounds of the Kremlin (the seat of the Soviet government) along with other heroes of the Bolshevik revolution. Reed was the only American and one of the few foreigners to be honored with a Kremlin burial.

John Reed's legacy

Rarely has a more controversial figure than John Reed arisen in the course of American history. He was considered a hero by social activists and a traitor by the political and business establishment. The gulf in perceptions of Reed's character only widened after his death.

In the 1920s and 1930s left-wing activists formed political protest organizations called John Reed clubs, named for their ideological leader. Reed's life and political pursuits were depicted in the 1981 movie *Reds,* starring Warren Beatty and Diane Keaton.

Sources

Books

Duke, David C. *John Reed.* Boston: Twayne Publishers, 1987.

Hamilton, Stacey. "Reed, John." *American National Biography.* Vol. 18. Edited by John A. Garraty and Mark C. Carnes. New York: Oxford University Press, 1999, pp. 268–70.

Rosenstone, Robert A. *Romantic Revolutionary: A Biography of John Reed.* New York: Alfred A. Knopf, 1975.

McGuire, William, and Leslie Wheeler. *American Social Leaders.* Santa Barbara, CA: ABC-CLIO, 1993.

Gloria Richardson

Born May 6, 1922
Baltimore, Maryland

Civil rights leader

Gloria Richardson was the controversial, charismatic, and fearless leader of the civil rights movement in Cambridge, Maryland. Her boldness in demanding complete equality for all of Cambridge's citizens, regardless of race, and her willingness to back up her words with actions, earned her the respect and admiration of many African Americans and the ire of many whites. Indeed, white residents of Cambridge tried twice to have Richardson committed, claiming she was insane. Often referred to as "General Richardson" in a civil rights struggle called the "Battle of Cambridge," Richardson advocated nonviolent direct action but did not dissuade her followers from taking up arms for self-defense.

Member of a prominent family

Richardson was born on May 6, 1922, in Baltimore, Maryland, the only child of John Edwards Hayes and Mabel Pauline St. Clair Hayes. Her family had been in Maryland for several generations, and her ancestors had been some of the state's first free blacks.

"The best way for Negroes across the country to gain freedom is through demonstrations to make it known that Negroes do not have everything they should under the U.S. Constitution. Everyone should get every bit of freedom he can get and get it now. We want it all, here and now!"

Gloria Richardson in a 1964 interview

Gloria Richardson.
Reproduced by permission of Corbis-Bettmann.

457

When Richardson was six years old, her family moved to Cambridge, Maryland. There Richardson's grandfather, Herbert Maynadier St. Clair, was on the city council. He was the second African American to be elected to the council, serving from 1912 to 1946. Nonetheless, he was not treated the same as the white council members. For example, St. Clair was not allowed to attend the annual city council banquet; instead, he was given a plate of food to eat at home.

Education, marriage, and divorce

Richardson attended Frederick Douglass High School (now Maces Lane High School), then went on to Howard University—a prominent, mostly black university in Washington, D.C. There she studied with some of the leading African American scholars and black-rights proponents of the time and received a bachelor of arts degree in sociology in 1942. Richardson then married a schoolteacher named Harry Richardson, had two daughters, and settled into the life of a homemaker. In 1958 the couple divorced. Soon thereafter Richardson moved back to Cambridge with her two daughters.

Entry into civil rights struggle

As a child Richardson had chosen to ignore the two-tiered social system that made African Americans second-class citizens. She adapted to her surroundings by pretending that racism and Jim Crow did not exist. (Jim Crow was the network of laws and customs that dictated the separation of the races on every level of society.) In the 1960s, however, as the fight for racial equality gained steam, Richardson changed her attitude toward societal injustice. At the same time, the white majority of Cambridge's citizens remained steadfastly opposed to social reform. (Cambridge in the early 1960s had 8,000 whites and 4,200 blacks.)

Richardson was swept up in the tide of change in 1962, when a group of young activists from the **Student Nonviolent Coordinating Committee** (SNCC; see entry) visited Cambridge and rallied African Americans to the cause of equal rights. "There was something direct," Richardson stated in a 1963 *Newsweek* interview, "something real about the way the kids waged nonviolent war. This was the first time I saw a vehicle I could work with." Richardson followed the lead of her daughter, Donna, into the movement, and soon rose to the fore.

Leads Cambridge Nonviolent Action Committee

In the wake of the civil rights activists' visit, African Americans in Cambridge formed the Cambridge Nonviolent Action Committee (CNAC; pronounced SEE-nack). Richardson became cochair, with Inez Grubb, of CNAC in June 1962. Richardson was a natural choice for the leadership position, since her family was financially independent and well-respected in the community, which would probably enable them to survive retaliation by the white business community. (In that era, African American activists commonly faced reprisals by white employers, lending institutions, utility companies, and other powerful interests, as a means of deterring civil rights involvement.)

Richardson's first task as CNAC leader was to poll Cambridge's African American residents to determine their greatest concerns. Richardson summarized the survey results and came up with a list of fifteen demands. Among the demands were nondiscrimination in employment (upwards of 50 percent of African Americans in Cambridge were unemployed at the time), access to adequate and affordable housing, school desegregation, police protection, and access to medical services. CNAC also pushed for the integration of stores, swimming pools, and other public facilities. CNAC was almost alone among civil rights groups at the time in including issues of economic justice among its demands, and it was the first large civil rights group to be led by a woman.

Initiates campaign for civil rights

CNAC kicked off its civil rights campaign in March 1963 by presenting the Cambridge city council with its list of demands. Cochairs Richardson and Grubb warned council members that if the complete integration of Cambridge did not occur immediately, CNAC would begin holding protests. When city council did not respond, CNAC made good on its threat. Several segregated facilities were targeted for pickets

1963: The Year of "Freedom Now"

In 1963 civil rights activism around the United States reached its peak. The slogan of the campaigns, which resounded through the streets everywhere, was "Freedom Now!" In addition to Cambridge, there were protest campaigns that year in Birmingham, Alabama; Gadsden and Pine Bluff, Alabama; Plaquemine, Louisiana; Nashville and Knoxville, Tennessee; Greensboro and Raleigh, North Carolina; Jackson, Mississippi; Savannah, Georgia; Danville, Virginia; and many other cities. During the spring and summer of 1963, there was a total of about 930 demonstrations in 115 cities across eleven southern states, resulting in the arrests of more than twenty thousand activists. The highlight of the year was the March on Washington for Jobs and Freedom, which drew a quarter of a million people to Washington, D.C., on August 28.

and sit-ins, including the city hall, the county courthouse, the Dorset Theater (Cambridge's only movie house, which would only seat African Americans in the back half of the balcony), the skating rink, and the jail. (Sit-ins are protests in which African American activists, sometimes join by whites, request service in a whites-only facility, then refuse to leave when denied service.) African Americans also began an economic boycott of downtown businesses. In the first seven weeks of demonstrations, eighty people were arrested—among them Richardson.

The arrested activists were brought to trial that May. In the proceedings, nicknamed the "Penny Trials," the protesters were found guilty. They were fined one penny each and given suspended sentences (meaning they served no jail time). The judge ridiculed the protesters' cause and singled out Richardson for special criticism, charging that her arrest had brought disgrace upon her family.

Undeterred, CNAC activists headed back to the streets. On a single day—May 14—sixty-two people were arrested in the theater lobby and in a restaurant. Among those taken into custody were three generations of St. Clair women: Mabel St. Clair Hayes (Richardson's mother), Richardson, and Donna Richardson (Richardson's daughter).

An uneasy peace

Following the mid-May arrests, the Committee on Interracial Understanding was established. The committee, comprised of city officials, white residents, and a judge, studied CNAC's demands and agreed to institute five of them: desegregation of public schools and public accommodations (such as stores, restaurants, and theaters); nondiscrimination in hiring in stores and factories (with a beginning goal of making work forces at least 10 percent African American); the construction of a low-income, public-housing project, as well as a study of sewers and sidewalks in African American neighborhoods; and an end to police brutality against African Americans (plus the appointment of an African American deputy sheriff).

Despite the promise of the reform, CNAC activists noticed no changes. Protest activity began anew on May 25, when twelve youths picketed the office of the Board of Education and were arrested. The youngsters were expelled from school; consequently, members of CNAC resumed the economic boycott and picketed downtown stores.

Segregationist groups then pressed to have the Public Accommodations Law, which was to have banned discrimination against minority groups throughout Maryland beginning June 2, put on hold pending a voter referendum. On May 31, Richardson appealed to U.S. Attorney General Robert F. Kennedy to investigate violations of constitutional rights in Cambridge. Kennedy did not respond. The promise of reform was unmasked as having been a cruel taunt.

The struggle intensifies

On June 10 the already tense situation in Cambridge escalated into violence. A fifteen-year-old girl named Dinez White, who had been arrested the previous month for praying outside a segregated bowling alley, was sentenced on that date to a correctional school for an undetermined length of time. The sentence provoked angry demonstrations on the part of Cambridge's African American community. Fires were set and bombs ignited, and two white men were shot in the chest. Fights broke out between whites and blacks. Armed African American men began patrolling their streets at night.

State troopers were sent into Cambridge three days later and sealed off entrances to the black ghetto. Maryland's governor declared a state of martial law and called in the National Guard. On June 15, some five hundred Maryland National Guardsmen were positioned on Cambridge streets. Curfews were established and demonstrations prohibited.

On July 8, the day the National Guard pulled out of Cambridge, a group of African American students held a sit-in in the segregated Dizzyland Restaurant—a frequent target of CNAC protests. The restaurant's owner broke an egg on the head of the group's white participant and poured water over him. The next day three whites were arrested for punching demonstrators, and the day after that civil rights protesters again sat in at the Dizzyland. The following day, July 11, demonstrators were brutally beaten inside the restaurant. Racial violence flared and the National Guard was called back to Cambridge.

Civil war in Cambridge?

During the halt in demonstrations (mandated by the reimposition of martial law), Richardson joined with other black and white leaders to find a solution to the conflict. On July 15, when returning to Cambridge from a race-relations conference sponsored by the governor in Annapolis, Maryland, Richardson and other African American leaders were arrested. They was released soon thereafter. Richardson then called for a halt in all demonstrations, to allow the Race Relations Committee of the Bar Association of Maryland an opportunity to find a solution.

The governor soon announced, however, that he was not giving the Bar Association authority to mediate the dispute. Richardson charged the white authorities with foot-dragging. At a meeting held at the Bethel A.M.E. Church on July 21, Richardson warned that Cambridge may be on the brink of civil war and called for President John F. Kennedy (1917–1963; president 1961–63) to intervene. "Unless something is achieved soon in Cambridge, then no one is going to be able to control these people who have been provoked by generations of segregation, by countless indignities—and now by uncontrollable white mobs in the streets," stated Richardson. " . . . Instead of progress, we have anarchy. . . . We live in a town where a man might be killed tomorrow, where civil war might break out next week."

Helps craft Treaty of Cambridge

On July 22, 1963, Richardson was invited to Washington, D.C., to work out a truce. The meeting with Robert F.

Kennedy (attorney general under his brother President Kennedy; 1925–1968), Burke Marshall (assistant attorney general for civil rights), and Robert Weaver (head of the Housing and Home Finance Agency) yielded an agreement that certain changes would occur in Cambridge: desegregation of public schools and hospitals; construction of public housing units for African Americans; provisions to end job discrimination; and desegregation of places of public accommodation. The agreement, called the Treaty of Cambridge, was endorsed by CNAC representatives and Cambridge city officials.

Loses deal in voter referendum

Shortly thereafter, what seemed like a "done deal" began to unravel. White Cambridge residents circulated petitions to subject the Treaty of Cambridge to a voter referendum. More than 25 percent of Cambridge residents signed the petitions, meaning that by law the measure would have to be put to a vote.

Richardson split with other African American leaders on how to treat the referendum. While ministers and other prominent African Americans were in favor of campaigning for the ballot measure's passage, Richardson urged African Americans to ignore the vote. She asserted that the rights outlined in the agreement were already constitutionally guaranteed to African Americans and should not be subject to voter approval. In the referendum, held October 1, the treaty was defeated by 274 votes. More than half of Cambridge's African American voters had abstained. Many people blamed Richardson for the measure's defeat.

Richardson and CNAC vindicated

The referendum was unable to stop the forces of social change. In late 1963 and 1964 several reforms came to Cambridge. Schools were desegregated, employment opportunities were opened up to African Americans, and the hospital and library were desegregated. Other forms of institutionalized racism were neutralized with the passage of the 1964 Civil Rights Act (this piece of legislation, signed on July 2, 1964, outlawed racial discrimination in education, voting, and public accommodations).

Richardson and CNAC's civil rights campaign were vindicated in January 1964. At that time the U.S. Civil Rights Commission released a forty-nine page report siding with the civil rights activists in the "Battle of Cambridge." The report criticized Maryland's governor and Cambridge's white political and business leaders for contributing to the hostilities and for creating unjust living conditions for African Americans.

Makes new life in New York City

Richardson's final political act in Cambridge was to protest a speech by Alabama governor George Wallace (Wallace was an ardent segregationist during the civil rights era). Richardson led a group of civil rights activists to the Fireman's Arena—a segregated skating rink that had been the target of numerous sit-ins—where Wallace had chosen to make his speech. The group was dispersed by tear gas, and Richardson and thirteen others were arrested.

In August 1964 Richardson resigned the leadership of CNAC and moved to New York City. She married Frank Dandridge, a freelance photographer whom she had met during the civil rights campaign. The relationship ended in divorce in 1973.

One of Richardson's first positions in New York City was assistant director for the National Council of Negro Women. "We're trying to develop a black women's movement cutting across ideologies and groups—one that centers on issues at the state and local level," Richardson told *Ebony* magazine in February 1974.

Activities in recent years

In the 1980s Richardson began working for the Human Resources division of New York City, and with the city's Department for the Aging. As the 1990s came to a close, Richardson (then in her late 70s) continued to live in a Manhattan apartment. She made frequent trips to see friends and family in Cambridge and her grandchildren in Washington, D.C.

"There were a lot of young people involved with the movement in the 1960s," stated Richardson in a 1998 newspaper interview. "I really wish something would jump-start the youth of today to get them involved. If they knew their history, they would be drawn into the struggle."

Sources

Books

Allen, Zita. *Black Women Leaders of the Civil Rights Movement.* New York: Franklin Watts, 1996, pp. 90–95.

Brock, Annette K. "Gloria Richardson." *Notable Black American Women.* Edited by Jessie Carney Smith. Detroit: Gale Research, Inc., 1992, pp. 938–40.

Crawford, Vicki L., Jacqueline Anne Rouse, and Barbara Woods, eds. *Women in the Civil Rights Movement: Trailblazers and Torchbearers, 1941–1965.* Brooklyn, NY: Carlson Publishing, Inc., 1990.

Giddings, Paula. *When and Where I Enter: The Impact of Black Women on Race and Sex in America.* New York: William Morrow & Company, 1984.

Thompson, Kathleen. "Richardson, Gloria St. Clair Hayes." *Black Women in America: An Historical Encyclopedia.* Vol. 2. Edited by Darlene Clark Hine. Brooklyn, NY: Carlson Publishing, Inc., 1993, pp. 980–82.

Articles

Coleman, Chrisena. "Rights Pioneer Looks Homeward." *Daily News.* (New York). February 8, 1998: 28.

"Gloria Richardson." *Newsweek.* August 5, 1963: 26–28.

"Gloria Richardson: Lady General of Civil Rights." *Ebony.* July 1964: 23+.

"Whatever Happened to . . . Gloria Richardson?" *Ebony.* February 1974: 138.

Paul Robeson

Born April 9, 1898
Princeton, New Jersey
Died January 23, 1976
Philadelphia, Pennsylvania

Human rights activist, actor, singer,
athlete, and lawyer

"[Paul Robeson] is without doubt today, as a person, the best known American on earth, to the largest number of human beings. . . . Only in his native land is he without honor or rights."

W. E. B. DuBois, speaking to a Harlem audience in the early 1950s

Paul Robeson.
Photograph by Carl Van Vechten. Reproduced by permission of the estate of Carl Van Vechten.

Paul Robeson, from the 1920s through the 1960s, dazzled the world with his extraordinary acting, singing, and athletic performances. Robeson made several visits to the Soviet Union at the height of his career and came to embrace communism (the theory of social organization based on the holding of all property in common). When Robeson returned to the United States in 1939 after living abroad for ten years, he campaigned against lynching (the extralegal execution of a person [usually an African American] accused of a crime or a violation of social mores, often by hanging, by a group of three or more people) and refused to perform for segregated (separated by race) audiences. His career was brought to a halt by the U.S. government and entertainment industry during the anticommunist hysteria of the 1950s.

Son of a runaway slave

Robeson was born on April 9, 1898, in Princeton, New Jersey. He was the youngest of five children of William Robeson, an escaped slave and minister, and Maria Robeson, a schoolteacher. Robeson's mother burned to death in a tragic accident when Robeson was just six years old. His father, who had put himself through Lincoln University, stressed the importance of education. William Robeson also taught his children to conduct themselves with dignity and courage in the face of racism.

All-American athlete in college

Robeson excelled at academics and athletics and upon graduation from high school was awarded a scholarship to Rutgers University in New Brunswick, New Jersey. During his years at Rutgers, from 1915 to 1919, Robeson was one of only two African American students. He did well in his studies, won many prizes in speech contests, and was named class valedictorian (the student with the best grades, who makes the graduation speech). Robeson also demonstrated great prowess as an athlete. Despite initial attempts by white athletes to bar Robeson's participation, he earned a total of twelve letters in track, football, baseball, and basketball. For two years Robeson received the designation "All-American" in football, meaning he was one of the best college athletes in the United States.

After graduation from Rutgers, Robeson headed for law school at Columbia University in New York. There he met and married Eslanda Cordozo Goode—a fellow student at Columbia who became an anthropologist, chemist, writer, and activist. (The couple had one son, named Paul, in 1927.) Robeson put himself through law school with the money he earned playing professional football on weekends. During his years in law school (1921–23) Robeson also acted in amateur theatrical productions.

Rises to international acclaim in theater

After earning his law degree, Robeson had a difficult time finding a firm willing to hire an African American lawyer. When he finally did find employment with a prestigious firm in New York City, he encountered more discrimination. Other lawyers refused to work with him and secretaries refused to take dictation from him.

Robeson left the profession in disgust and, encouraged by his wife, attempted to launch an acting career. From his first roles, Robeson was a hit. Before long he was gracing stages on Broadway, in New York, and at London's Savoy Theatre (Eng-

land). He received high acclaim after starring in two plays by Eugene O'Neill: *The Emperor Jones* and *All God's Chillun Got Wings*. A reviewer in *Newsweek* called Robeson "thoroughly eloquent, impressive, and convincing."

Robeson's performances, both in classical and contemporary plays, drew huge audiences. One of his greatest roles was as the title character in William Shakespeare's tragedy *Othello*. His performance as Othello in New York in 1943 drew remarkably long and energetic ovations; the play was the longest-running Broadway production of a Shakespearean play. Robeson became recognized as the world's leading African American actor. He also appeared in at least a dozen films.

Even as an international celebrity, however, Robeson was not immune from the barbs of racism. As an African American man in pre–civil rights times, Robeson was forced to take the freight elevator and enter through the back doors of many establishments. He was barred entirely from several restaurants and hotels. In one instance a passer-by spat upon a white woman with whom he was walking (the mixing of black men with white women was strictly forbidden by the social mores of the time).

Sings for racial and economic justice

Robeson initiated his career as a singer in 1925, when he presented a concert of all-Negro spirituals (religious songs about freedom and slavery) and songs about working people. Over time he incorporated songs from other minority cultures and other nations. He sang in several languages, including Chinese, Yiddish, and Russian. (Robeson mastered more than twenty languages during his lifetime.) Robeson also sang in musical theater productions. One of his most popular performances was the singing of "Ol' Man River" in the musical *Showboat*.

Robeson made a point of singing not just to well-to-do concert-goers, but also to audiences of common people. In his songs he embraced the causes of racial and economic justice.

Spends decade abroad

In 1928 Robeson moved with his wife and son to London, England. In his ten years living abroad Robeson frequently traveled through Europe. He met many influential socialists (people who believe that the means of production should not be controlled by owners, but by the community as a whole) and African nationalists (African citizens who support the independence of their nations from European colonizers). Among his friends were independence leaders **Kwame Nkrumah** (1909–1972; became the first prime minister of Ghana in 1957; see entry), Jomo Kenyatta (1889–1978; became president of Kenya in 1964), and Jawaharlal Nehru (1889–1964; became first prime minister of India in 1947).

Visits Soviet Union and embraces communism

In 1934, at the invitation of the filmmaker Sergei Eisenstein, Robeson made his first of many visits to the Soviet Union. Robeson explored the workings of the socialist system by visiting hospitals, children's centers, and factories. In the evenings he attended theater and opera performances. Robeson came to the conclusion that the Soviet Union was free from racial prejudice. He felt a personal connection, as a descendant of slaves, with the Russian citizens—the descendants of serfs. The way Robeson saw it, the Russians had survived feudalism just as African Americans had survived slavery.

Robeson demonstrated his commitment to communism during the Spanish Civil War (1936–39): the battle in which the opposition Nationalist forces attempted to topple by force the ruling Republican government. The Republicans—comprised of urban workers, farm workers, students, much of the educated middle class, and some sixty thousand sympathetic individuals from around the world who comprised the International Brigades—were adherents of communism and anarchism (the latter being the opposition to all forms of centralized government). The Nationalists—comprised of military and church leaders, large landholders, businessmen, and the fascist governments of Italy and Nazi Germany—were adherents of fascism (a form of government characterized by a dictator with complete power, the forcible suppression of opposition, and the promotion of nationalism and racism).

Robeson sang and spoke at a fund-raising rally for the Republicans in 1937 in England. "Like every true artist, I have longed to see my talent contributing in an unmistakably clear manner to the cause of humanity," Robeson stated. "The liberation of Spain from the oppression of fascist reactionaries is not a private matter of the Spaniards, but the common cause of all advanced and progressive humanity."

Returns to United States; campaigns for rights of African Americans

Robeson returned to the United States with his wife and young son in 1939. His years abroad had transformed him into a steadfast human-rights and civil-rights activist. Robeson took up many issues upon his return, from segregation to lynching. He refused to sing in theaters that only allowed whites or made African Americans sit in a balcony. He joined picket lines in front of the White House protesting racial segregation. Robeson also spoke before Congress, demanding that African American athletes be allowed to play on professional sports teams (it was not until 1947 that the first African American baseball player,

Robeson Testifies Before HUAC

Robeson was called to testify before the House Committee on Un-American Activities (HUAC) on June 12, 1956. (HUAC, which was established as a special committee in 1938 and became a regular, standing committee of the House of Representatives in 1945, held hearings from 1947 to 1957 to expose alleged communists. Their "witch-hunt," as it came to be known, yielded only a handful of dubious convictions of individuals for advocating the overthrow of the United States government. In response to HUAC's question: "Are you now a member of the Communist Party?" Robeson replied, "Would you like to come to the ballot box when I vote and take out the ballot and see?" He would give no further response to the question.

"I am not being tried for whether I am a Communist," Robeson told the committee, "I am being tried for fighting for the rights of my people, who are still second class citizens in the U.S. of America."

When Robeson was asked why he had returned to the United States instead of remaining in the Soviet Union, he replied, "Because my father was a slave and my people died to build this country, and I am going to stay here and have a part of it just like you. And no fascist-minded people will drive me from it. Is that clear?"

Jackie Robinson, was admitted to the major leagues). Given that the civil rights movement in America did not gain momentum until the mid-1950s, Robeson was truly ahead of his time.

Robeson continued to voice his support for the Soviet Union and for communism. During World War II (1939–45) he implored African Americans not to fight if the United States went to war against the Soviet Union. Robeson claimed that the interests of African Americans were more in line with the Soviet Union (which practiced racial equality) than with the United States (which practiced racial discrimination).

Blacklisted during period of anticommunist hysteria

Robeson's civil rights activities, as well as his public support for the Soviet Union and communism, came to the attention of U.S. government officials. Beginning in the late 1940s Robeson was investigated as a possible threat to U.S. security. Robeson was not alone—during the decade of anti-communist hysteria, approximately six million Americans were investigated by administrative agencies and legislative committees.

In 1950 the State Department revoked Robeson's passport, thus depriving him of the right to perform for international audiences. To make matters worse, entertainment industry officials placed Robeson on a "blacklist," meaning that they prohibited Robeson—along with hundreds of other people in the entertainment industry they believed were sympathetic to communism—from working in theater, movies, and television. In addition, Robeson's name was removed from the list of "All American" athletes. In the early 1950s Robeson's yearly income plummeted steeply from his 1947 earnings of $104,000 to a mere $2,000.

Political turmoil takes personal toll

Robeson had his passport restored in 1957, after the Supreme Court concluded that his constitutional rights had been violated. Even though Robeson's days of government harassment were over, American media and entertainment industries continued to shun him. In 1958, when Robeson published his autobiography, *Here I Stand,* major news sources refused to review it or even to include it in their lists of new publications.

The years of persecution and silencing had produced a severe depression in Robeson. "Pariah status was utterly alien to the gregarious Robeson," wrote journalist Dennis Drabble in *Smithsonian* magazine. "He became depressed at the loss of contact with audiences and friends, and suffered a series of breakdowns that left him withdrawn. . . . "

Robeson spent the last seven years of his career traveling among the Soviet Union, Europe, Australia, and the United States. His international performances, although infrequent, drew huge audiences. Robeson returned to the United States in 1963, in poor health, and settled into retirement in Philadelphia, Pennsylvania. His wife died in 1965. Robeson succumbed to a stroke on January 23, 1976. Robeson's life was characterized by John Patrick Diggins, writing for *The Nation*, as "at once an American triumph and an American tragedy."

Sources

Books

Duberman, Martin Bauml. *Paul Robeson*. New York: Alfred A. Knopf, 1989.

Greenfield, Eloise. *Paul Robeson*. New York: Thomas Y. Crowell Company, 1975.

Robeson, Paul. *Here I Stand*. Boston, Beacon Press, 1958.

Smallwood, David, et al. *Profiles of Great African Americans*. Lincolnwood, IL: Publications International, Ltd., 1996, pp. 150–54.

Articles

Jordan, June. "A Shout-Out for Paul Robeson." *Essence*. November 1998: 212.

Web Sites

"Paul Robeson." DISCovering Biography. The Gale Group. [Online] Available http://galenet.gale.com (accessed January 27, 2000).

Jo Ann Gibson Robinson

Born April 17, 1912
Culloden, Georgia

Civil rights activist and teacher

> "Boycotting taught me courage. The memory of the thousands of boycotters, walking in hot and cold weather, in rain, sleet, and sunshine, for thirteen long months, makes me feel ever so humble. These people inspired me to refuse to accept what was wrongfully imposed upon me."

Jo Ann Gibson Robinson in The Montgomery Bus Boycott and the Women Who Started It.

Jo Ann Gibson Robinson was one of the most important leaders of the 1955–56 Montgomery bus boycott. She had been standing up for the rights of African Americans for years before the boycott began. And her organization, the Women's Political Council, had made preparations for a bus boycott months in advance of the arrest of Rosa Parks (1913–; see box in Highlander Education Center entry)—the spark that set the boycott in motion.

The best-known leader of the Montgomery bus boycott was **Martin Luther King, Jr.** (see entry). Yet Robinson, like other behind-the-scenes organizers (most of them women), deserves recognition for her invaluable contribution to the success of the event that began the civil rights movement.

Childhood in rural Georgia

Jo Ann Gibson was born in rural Georgia, near the town of Culloden, on April 17, 1912. She was the youngest of twelve children (six boys and six girls) born to Owen Boston Gibson and Dollie Webb Gibson. After Gibson's father died in

1918, she went with her mother and some of her siblings (the older ones had already married and moved out) to live with an older brother in Macon, Georgia.

Gibson attended segregated schools in Macon and graduated valedictorian of her high school senior class. She then became the only one of her siblings to go on to college. Because of her good grades, Gibson was awarded a scholarship to Georgia State College in Fort Valley. After graduating with a bachelor of science degree, she became a schoolteacher in Macon.

In Macon Gibson met and married Wilbur Robinson. They had one child who died in infancy. Overcome with grief, Jo Ann Gibson Robinson (as she was called after taking her husband's name) found it impossible to continue her marriage. She left her husband and five-year teaching career in Macon and moved to Atlanta, Georgia, for more schooling.

The road to Montgomery

Robinson attended graduate school at Atlanta University and earned a master's degree in English language and literature. She then moved to New York City and completed one year of a doctoral program in English at Columbia University's Teachers College. Robinson next transferred to the University of Southern California in Los Angeles and went through one more semester of graduate school.

Robinson then returned to teaching, but at the college level. Her first position was at Mary Allen College in Crockett, Texas. There she served as chairperson of the English department. In 1949, at the age of thirty-seven, Robinson was offered and accepted a teaching position in the English department of Alabama State College, in Montgomery.

Robinson's move to Montgomery represented a critical juncture in her life's work, and led to her becoming an activist. Upon her arrival in Montgomery, Robinson met several teachers who were members of the Women's Political Council (WPC)—an organization of African American women, formed in 1946, that promoted educational opportunities for African American youth and encouraged African Americans to register to vote. (Prior to the passage of the Voting Rights Bill in 1965, blacks in the South were kept from registering to vote by legal requirements and threats of violence.) Robinson's new friends

Robinson's Letter to Montgomery's Mayor

Jo Ann Gibson Robinson sent the following letter (dated May 21, 1954) on behalf of the Women's Political Council to Mayor W. A. Gayle of Montgomery, Alabama. This letter was delivered six months before Rosa Parks' arrest touched off the Montgomery bus boycott.

Dear Sir:

The Women's Political Council is very grateful to you and the City Commissioners for the hearing you allowed our representatives during the month of March, 1954, when the "city-bus-fare-increase case" was being reviewed.

There were several things the Council asked for:

1. *A city law that would make it possible for Negroes to sit from back toward front, and whites from front toward back until all the seats are taken;*

2. *That Negroes not be asked or forced to pay fare at front and go to the rear of the bus to enter;*

3. *That busses stop at every corner in residential sections occupied by Negroes as they do in communities where whites reside.*

We are happy to report that busses have been stopping at more corners now in some sections where Negroes live than previously. However, the same practices in seating and boarding the bus continue.

had no problem persuading her to join the WPC. Robinson also became a member of the Dexter Avenue Baptist Church. A few years after Robinson moved to Montgomery, that church hired a new pastor—Martin Luther King, Jr.

Experiences mistreatment on Montgomery bus

In December 1949, just three months after her arrival in Montgomery, Robinson happily prepared to spend the holidays with friends and relatives in Ohio. She took a city bus to meet a friend with whom she planned to drive to the airport. Robinson's pleasant musings, however, were disturbed shortly after she boarded the bus.

She had taken a seat in the fifth row (the bus contained two other passengers; a white woman at the front and a black man at the rear). The bus driver ordered Robinson to move back farther toward the rear of the bus. Robinson was not aware immediately that she was being addressed. The driver

Mayor Gayle, three-fourths of the riders of these public conveyances are Negroes. If Negroes did not patronize them, they could not possibly operate.

More and more of our people are already arranging with neighbors and friends to ride to keep from being insulted and humiliated by bus drivers.

There has been talk from twenty-five or more local organizations of planning a city-wide boycott of busses. We, sir, do not feel that forceful measures are necessary in bargaining for a convenience which is right for all bus passengers. We, the Council, believe that when this matter has been put before you and the Commissioners, that agreeable terms can be met in a quiet and unostensible manner to the satisfaction of all concerned.

Many of our Southern cities in neighboring states have practiced the policies we seek without incident whatsoever. Atlanta, Macon and Savannah in Georgia have done this for years. Even Mobile, in our own state, does this and all the passengers are satisfied.

Please consider this plea, and if possible, act favorably upon it, for even now plans are being made to ride less, or not at all, on our buses. We do not want this.

Respectfully yours,
The Women's Political Council
Jo Ann Robinson, President

then approached her, with his hand held back as if prepared to strike, and yelled, "Get up from there!"

"I leaped to my feet, afraid he would hit me, and ran to the front door to get off the bus . . ." Robinson wrote in her memoir *The Montgomery Bus Boycott and the Women Who Started It.* "It suddenly occurred to me that I was supposed to go to the back door to get off, not the front! However, I was too upset, frightened, and tearful to move. . . . Then the driver opened the front door, and I stumbled off the bus and started walking back to the college. Tears blinded my vision; waves of humiliation inundated me."

Takes over reins of Women's Political Council

Robinson never forgot her experience on the bus. She learned that she was not alone—that African Americans were commonly subjected to such humiliation on city buses.

In 1950 Robinson took over as president of the WPC. She changed the WPC into an activist organization dedicated to protesting the poor treatment of Montgomery's African American citizens. Her pet issue remained the bus system's policy of racial segregation. It irked Robinson that African Americans, who formed the overwhelming majority of bus ridership, were treated with contempt by bus drivers. She also believed that African Americans had the power to make the bus company change.

Prepares for bus boycott

From 1950 to 1955 the WPC, in Robinson's words, "prepared to stage a bus boycott when the time was ripe and the people were ready." Robinson and other WPC members laid the groundwork while waiting for the opportune moment—an incident around which they could rally all African American Montgomery residents—to begin a boycott.

One way in which the WPC prepared for the boycott was to create a leaflet that only needed a meeting time and place to be filled in. The leaflet read: "Another Negro woman has been arrested and put in jail because she refused to give up her seat on the bus for a white person to sit down. . . . Negroes have rights, too, for if Negroes did not ride the buses, they could not operate. Don't ride the buses to work, to town, to school, or anywhere." In the early 1950s the WPC also appealed to the city commissioners, the mayor, and the bus company to change the back-of-the-bus policy.

Organizes initial stages of bus boycott

On December 1, 1955, another black Montgomery resident was harassed on a city bus. That resident—a forty-two-year-old tailor's assistant (and secretary of the Montgomery NAACP) named Rosa Parks (see box in **Highlander Research and Education Center** entry)—refused to give up her seat to a white man and was arrested. News of Parks's arrest quickly reached the WPC.

Robinson instinctively knew that Parks's arrest was the ideal incident around which to rally African American citizens against injustice on city buses. Before Parks had even left the police station, Robinson had called a group of volunteers to

The Montgomery Bus Boycott

On December 1, 1955, a tailor's assistant named Rosa Parks made a quiet stand against racism. She refused a bus driver's order to give up her seat on a city bus to a white man and was arrested. In response to Parks's arrest—as well as the indignities that other black bus riders endured daily—the Women's Political Council (WPC) and the National Association for the Advancement of Colored People (NAACP) announced the beginning of a boycott of city buses by African Americans.

A new organization called the Montgomery Improvement Association (MIA) was formed to coordinate the boycott. The MIA selected a twenty-six-year-old minister named **Martin Luther King, Jr.,** (see entry) to be its president. King inspired Montgomery's African American populace to continue the boycott until African American riders would no longer be forced to give up their seats to whites. The boycotters also demanded more respectful treatment of blacks by bus drivers and the hiring of African American drivers.

Fifty-thousand African American Montgomerians honored the boycott for its duration. While some boycotters reached their destinations on foot, others rode in one of the city's 210 African American-owned taxicabs (African American cab-drivers charged the same ten-cent fare as buses during the boycott). Boycott organizers also coordinated carpools to get people to and from work. African American postal workers devised transportation routes based on their knowledge of city streets. Carpools were run by volunteer drivers, including several white women. Many people donated the use of their cars.

The boycott lasted 382 days and was ultimately successful. On December 20, 1956, the Montgomery City Lines bus company was served with a court order to abandon its policy of racial segregation.

pick up the leaflets the next morning. Robinson stayed up all that night copying leaflets. By seven o'clock the next evening, thirty-five thousand leaflets had been distributed around the city's black neighborhoods. The leaflets called people to a meeting that night, at which the Montgomery bus boycott (see box) was launched.

When the Montgomery Improvement Organization (MIA)—an organization headed by the city's black ministers, with Martin Luther King, Jr., at the helm—was formed to coordinate the boycott, Robinson was placed on the MIA's executive committee. Robinson doggedly worked throughout the boycott's thirteen months: organizing carpools, giving rides to boycotters during her off-work hours, and editing the monthly *MIA Newsletter* (the purpose of which was to keep participants and supporters informed of the boycott's progress).

Faces police harassment

Many leaders of the Montgomery bus boycott were harassed by policemen or white vigilantes, and the homes of Martin Luther King, Jr., and NAACP chairman E. D. Nixon were bombed. Robinson became a target of harassment in February 1956. One night that month a squad car pulled up to Robinson's house and an officer heaved a large stone through Robinson's picture window. Robinson boarded up the window and left it that way for the duration of the boycott.

Later in February, Robinson's home was again visited by policemen. Two officers poured acid on Robinson's car, creating holes in the roof, fenders, and hood. After that attack, the governor of Alabama ordered police protection at the homes of boycott leaders.

A hard-won victory

On November 13, 1956, the Supreme Court sided with the boycotters in ruling that segregation on public transportation systems was unconstitutional. On December 21, 1956, Montgomery City Lines was served with a court order to abandon its policy of racial segregation. The boycott had succeeded.

Robinson reminisced about the end of the boycott in her memoir *The Montgomery Bus Boycott and the Women Who Started It*. "After the verdict sank in, the initial outbursts subsided, tears were wiped away, voices grew calm," Robinson wrote. "In a few minutes the outward emotions disappeared, to be replaced by a prayerful attitude. Silent prayers of thanksgiving were uttered. A calm serenity spread over most faces. . . .

"All those years of inhuman suffering, of brutality, arrests, and fines [were over]. The victory, however, brought no open festivities, no public rejoicing in the streets, no crowds milling on corners or around the leaders' homes. Too many people had suffered too much to rejoice. Too many people had lost their jobs."

Leaves Montgomery

In the summer of 1960, after eleven years as a faculty member, Robinson decided it was time to leave Alabama State College. She resigned along with several other activist-professors who, in the aftermath of the boycott, had come under intense scrutiny by a special investigative board of the Alabama legislature. Robinson accepted a position as head of the English department at Grambling College in Grambling, Louisiana.

After a year in her new job, Robinson was offered a position teaching English in the Los Angeles public schools. Since she had experienced feelings of loneliness and isolation in Louisiana, she jumped at the opportunity to be with old friends in California. Robinson taught in Los Angeles until her retirement in 1976. Her teaching career had spanned thirty-five years and five different states: Georgia, Texas, Alabama, Louisiana, and California.

Robinson has remained active in retirement. She volunteers at a child care center and with voter registration drives. She is a member of the League of Women Voters, the Alpha Gamma Omega chapter of the Alpha Kappa Alpha Sorority, and the Angel City chapter of Links, the Black Women's Alliance. In 1989 Robinson was honored by the Southern Association for Women Historians for her 1987 memoir *The Montgomery Bus Boycott and the Women Who Started It.*

Sources

Books

Allen, Zita. *Black Women Leaders of the Civil Rights Movement.* New York: Franklin Watts, 1996, pp. 55–67.

Carson, Clayborne, et al., eds. *Eyes on the Prize Reader and Guide: America's Civil Rights Years.* New York: Penguin Books, 1991, pp. 41–42.

Crawford, Vicki L., Jacqueline Anne Rouse, and Barbara Woods, eds. *Women in the Civil Rights Movement: Trailblazers and Torchbearers, 1941–1965 .* Brooklyn, NY: Carlson Publishing, Inc., 1990.

Elliott, Derek. "Jo Ann Gibson Robinson." *Notable Black American Women.* Vol. 2. Edited by Jessie Carney Smith. Detroit: Gale Research, Inc., 1996, pp. 562–64.

Giddings, Paula. *When and Where I Enter: The Impact of Black Women on Race and Sex in America.* New York: William Morrow and Company, 1984, pp. 261–67.

Hine, Darlene Clark, and Kathleen Thompson. *A Shining Thread of Hope: The History of Black Women in America.* New York: Broadway Books, 1998, pp. 273–76.

Robinson, Jo Ann Gibson. *The Montgomery Bus Boycott and the Women Who Started It.* Knoxville: University of Tennessee Press, 1987.

Stein, R. Conrad. *The Story of the Montgomery Bus Boycott* Chicago: Children's Press, 1986.

Articles
Thornton, Jeannye. "'I'm Not Going to Ride the Bus.'" *U.S. News and World Report.* December 11, 1995: 52+.

Oscar Romero

Born August 15, 1917
Ciudad Barrios, El Salvador
Died March 24, 1980
San Salvador, El Salvador

Former Archbishop of San Salvador
and human rights activist

Oscar Romero was a martyr for the causes of social justice, human rights, and peace. He was assassinated for his willingness to speak out against the intimidation and killings of civilians by the Salvadoran armed forces. Romero's selfless crusade earned him the love and admiration of El Salvador's poor majority. Romero's assassination, which was later revealed to have been ordered by a high-ranking official of the Salvadoran government, focused world attention on the tiny, war-torn Central American republic.

Grows up in remote village

Oscar Arnulfo Romero y Galdamez was born on August 15, 1917, in the village of Ciudad Barrios. His hometown was in the mountainous province of San Miguel, in the northeast of El Salvador. Romero was one of eight children born to Santos Romero and Guadalupe de Jesus Galdamez. Santos Romero was the town postmaster and manager of the telegraph office, which he ran out of his home. All of the Romero children helped deliver letters and telegrams.

"In the name of God, and in the name of this suffering people, whose laments rise to heaven each day more tumultuous, I beg you, I beseech you, I order you in the name of God: Stop the repression!"

Archbishop Oscar Romero in one of his last sermons.

Oscar Romero.
Reproduced by permission of Arte Publico Press Archives, University of Houston.

Romero was a serious student. He attended public schools through the third grade (the highest grade offered). From that time until the age of twelve, he was educated by a private tutor. For the following year he worked as an apprentice to a carpenter.

Religious training

At the age of thirteen Romero left his home to undergo religious training in nearby San Miguel. Seven years later he entered the Jesuit-run national seminary in the capital city, San Salvador. Romero completed his studies at the Gregorian University in Rome, Italy. He was ordained a priest on April 4, 1942, at the age of twenty-four.

Romero then returned to his homeland, where he conducted religious services first in Ciudad Barrios and then in the town of Anamoros. In January 1944 Romero was assigned to be secretary of the diocese in San Miguel. He remained there for twenty-three years. Romero's duties in that position included tending to the spiritual needs of parishioners, teaching catechism classes, acting as secretary to the bishop, overseeing the seminary, and editing the newsletter of the diocese. Romero also visited prison inmates and coordinated the distribution of food to poor people.

Rises in church hierarchy

Romero was given the title Monsignor in April 1967 and several months later named secretary-general of the national bishops' conference. His new position required that he move to San Salvador. Romero was promoted again in 1970, this time to bishop.

For two years beginning in 1975 Romero lived in the town of Santiago de Maria. There he was exposed to the injustices suffered by the common people at the hands of the military (a military government had been in place in El Salvador for decades). He also witnessed the growing movement for social justice. Romero, however, refused to get involved in political affairs. In the diocese newsletter he editorialized against priests becoming political activists.

Named archbishop

In 1977 Romero was given the church's highest ranking religious designation: archbishop. At the time, there was increasing civil strife throughout the nation. Peasants had formed unions (despite the illegality of the organizations) to demand redistribution of land. Land was concentrated in the hands of a few wealthy families, known as the oligarchy. In the 1950s and 1960s, the armed forces, at the behest of the oligarchy, had taken over peasant land so that wealthy Salvadorans could increase their production of coffee, cotton, and cattle for export.

Many peasants in the late 1970s were joining armed opposition groups (in 1980 those groups united as the Farabundo Martí Front for National Liberation—known by its Spanish acronym FMLN). At the same time, military rulers had unleashed a brutal campaign of repression against peasants and their supporters—among them Jesuit priests and lay workers.

Romero, who had a reputation as a conservative and as one unwilling to question the authority of the church or the government, had been the oligarchy's choice for archbishop. Romero's ordination was a lavish affair. Wealthy Salvadorans promised to build him a palace. Before long, however, Romero would decide to align himself with the poor. He refused the promised palace in favor of a small room next to the sacristy in the Divine Providence Hospital.

Condemns killings of civilians

In February 1977, just days after Romero became archbishop, one military-backed, conservative president succeeded another in an election marred by fraud. Massive strikes and demonstrations were held in San Salvador to demand honest elections. A group of forty thousand to sixty thousand protesters occupied a park called Plaza Libertad for three days. The occupation ended violently when soldiers in tanks fired on the crowd, killing some three hundred people.

Romero was pulled into the conflict in early March, when he was assigned to read a statement prepared by El Salvador's bishops condemning the killings. The day before Romero was to deliver the statement at a morning mass, however, he learned that the military had killed a Jesuit priest named Rutilio Grande and two of Grande's parishioners.

Romero Appeals for End to U.S. Aid

In February 1980 Romero called upon President Jimmy Carter (1924–; president 1977–81) to stop the flow of U.S. military aid to El Salvador. "We are fed up with weapons and bullets," Romero wrote in a letter.

The next month Romero again pleaded for an end to U.S. support of the Salvadoran military. In a letter to Carter that was made public by the U.S. government only in 1993, Romero wrote that the American contribution, "instead of promoting greater justice and peace in El Salvador, will without a doubt sharpen the injustice and repression against the organizations of the people which repeatedly have been struggling to gain respect for their most fundamental human rights."

President Carter, and later Presidents Ronald Reagan (1911–; president 1981–89) and George Bush (1924–; president 1989–93), ignored Romero's pleas. Between 1980 and 1991 the U.S. supported the Salvadoran military with about $4 billion.

Grande, who was a friend of Romero's, had helped organize the first workers' strike at a sugar mill north of San Salvador.

Romero read the bishops' statement on March 13, after which he conducted funeral services for Grande and his companions. The funeral was attended by a crowd that overflowed the church and continued into the plaza and street. The event marked a turning point in Romero's thinking. After that he found it impossible to remain silent about the injustices occurring across his homeland.

Intensifies opposition to continuing atrocities

Romero demanded an investigation into the death of Grande, stating that the church would boycott all government events until answers were provided. And to commemorate the lives of Grande and other Salvadorans killed by the military, Romero ordered all Catholic schools closed for three days.

Romero's demands for answers and an end to military terror fell upon deaf ears. As Romero learned of the increasing violence and repression against opponents of the government, he lost faith that he could negotiate with the administration.

Romero became a spokesperson for poor Salvadorans. In his Sunday services, which were carried over radio throughout the nation, he denounced the atrocities against his fellow citizens and called upon the army and government to respect human rights. In the newsletter of the archdiocese, Romero listed the names of people who had been arrested and disappeared while in military custody.

Repression increases against clergy members

Government officials and wealthy conservatives accused Romero and other clergy members of being subversives (those who attempt to overthrow the government) and communists (those who support a social system based on the holding of all property in common). Such labeling had serious repercussions for many religious personnel. Priests and lay people were arrested, tortured, murdered, or ordered to leave the country.

In May 1977 a church in the town of Aguilares (where Grande had organized the strike) was attacked by a military unit and occupied for several weeks. Soldiers gunned down numerous parishioners. And in June of the same year a military death squad ordered all Jesuits to leave the country or be killed. Military units throughout the nation were committing unspeakable atrocities in their effort to squelch the land-reform movement.

In July 1977 Romero boycotted the inauguration of the president who had prevailed in the fraudulent election. At the

The El Mozote Massacre

In December 1981, just one-and-a-half years after the killing of Oscar Romero, the El Mozote [pronounced el mo-ZO-tay] massacre took place. In what was arguably the most grizzly episode of the Salvadoran civil war (1979–91), armed forces killed about a thousand villagers, mostly women and children. Of the 794 victims whose remains were identified, the majority were children.

The killings were carried out over a three-day period beginning December 11, by an elite, U.S.-trained military unit called the Atlacatl battalion. According to a report by Tutela Legal, the human rights office of the Catholic Archdiocese of San Salvador, victims were summarily lined up and gunned down. The civilians killed in the massacre were from a group of villages (one of them called El Mozote) in the remote province of Morazan.

The massacre was reported by Raymond Bonner of the *New York Times* in a front-page story on January 27, 1982. The U.S. State Department, however, vigorously denied that a massacre had taken place. In fact, the day after the story appeared President Ronald Reagan gave El Salvador high marks for human rights and approved more U.S. aid to the Salvadoran military. The State Department actually worked to discredit Bonner and pressured the *Times* to remove Bonner from his Central America beat.

In 1993 the United Nations Truth Commission accused the U.S. government of having covered up the massacre. Four years later, Tutela Legal called for compensation for the families of victims of the El Mozote massacre.

same time, he became even bolder in his denunciation of the forces that sought to terrorize the peasantry into submission and in his calls for a peaceful resolution to the country's conflict. (Romero also criticized the use of violence by armed groups opposing the government.) Romero's calls for human rights and economic justice were met with death threats by the armed forces.

Receives international recognition

In addition to being widely respected and admired by his own people, Romero was internationally recognized for his

Monument erected in memory of those killed in the El Mozote Massacre being cleaned. *Reproduced by permission of AP/Wide World Photos.*

defense of human rights. In 1978 he was granted an honorary doctorate by Georgetown University in Washington, D.C. The following year he was nominated for a Nobel Peace Prize. Those honors brought El Salvador's human rights abuses to the attention of the world.

Injustices continue under new regime

In October 1979 the military government was overthrown in a coup by junior officers of the Salvadoran army. A group of rulers, called a junta [pronounced HOON-tah], was installed. The five-man junta consisted of civilians—both reformers and conservatives—and military officials. Immediately, U.S. aid was sent to bolster the Salvadoran government and armed forces.

Romero, wisely, looked upon the new government with apprehension. Within three months of the new government's formation, the reformers in the junta, their voices having been silenced, resigned and joined the opposition movement. Repression against peasants and clergy increased (more than one thousand people each month were killed during the junta's first year). Romero began receiving death threats on a regular basis.

Assassinated while celebrating mass

In early 1980 Romero began to recognize the very real possibility that his outspokenness would cost him his life. He prophesied his death in an interview just two weeks before he was gunned down: "I have often been threatened with death . . . as a Christian, I do not believe in death without resurrection. If I am killed, I shall arise again in the Salvadoran people. . . . Let my blood be a seed of freedom and a sign that hope will soon be a reality. Let my death, if it is accepted by God, be for my people's liberation and as a witness of hope in the future."

In one of his final homilies, on March 22, 1980, Romero called upon soldiers to refuse orders to kill their own countrymen. "No soldier is obliged to obey an order contrary to the law of God," Romero stated. "It is time that you come to your senses and obey your conscience rather than follow sinful commands."

On March 24, 1980, Romero was fired upon and killed by a masked gunman while conducting mass in a small chapel in San Salvador. He was sixty-two years old. His final words were, "May God have mercy on the assassins."

As the news of Romero's killing spread, shock and outrage rippled through El Salvador and the rest of the world. The tragedy of Romero's death was compounded at his funeral when gunmen fired upon the fifty thousand mourners, killing about one hundred.

U.N. Truth Commission identifies Romero's killers

Romero's murder was investigated, and his killers identified, in 1992 by the United Nations' Truth Commission. The commission was established as part of the 1991 agreement ending El Salvador's twelve-year-long civil war. (Between 1979 and 1991, seventy-five thousand civilians were killed—most of them by the armed forces.)

The Truth Commission determined that Romero's assassination had been ordered by Roberto D'Aubisson, a former army major and founder of El Salvador's conservative ruling Nationalist Republican Alliance party (ARENA). D'Aubisson (who died of cancer in 1992) was alleged to have hired his associate, Alvaro Savaria, to carry out the killing.

In 1999 statues of Romero and nine other twentieth-century Christian martyrs (among them **Martin Luther King, Jr., 1929–1968; see entry**) were erected on the grounds of London's (England) Westminster Abbey.

Sources

Books
Brockman, James R. *The Word Remains: A Life of Oscar Romero.* Maryknoll, NY: Orbis Books, 1982.

Gay, Kathlyn, and Martin K. Gay. *Heroes of Conscience: A Biographical Dictionary.* Santa Barbara, CA: ABC-CLIO, 1996, pp. 327–29.

Articles
Alder, Daniel. "Salvadoran Court Seeks U.S. Extradition." *United Press International.* May 24, 1994.

Kenyon, Karen. "20th Century Martyrs at Westminster Abbey." *British Heritage.* February–March 1999: 15.

Malcolm, Teresa. "Mass Commemorates Massacre." *National Catholic Reporter.* December 26, 1997: 9.

Neier, Aryeh. "Watching Rights." *The Nation.* December 16, 1991: 767.

"Salvador Archbishop Assassinated." *New York Times.* March 25, 1980.

Other
Morrissey, Michael. *El Salvador: Why Are We Fighting a War Against the Hungry?* (Pamphlet.) San Francisco: Institute for Food and Development Policy, 1983.

Romero. (Videorecording). John Duigan, Director. Trimark Home Video: 1989.

Augusto Sandino.
Reproduced by permission of Corbis Corporation (Bellevue).

Augusto C. Sandino

**Born May 18, 1894
Niquinohomo, Nicaragua
Died February 21, 1934
Managua, Nicaragua**

Nicaraguan revolutionary leader

"Patria libre o morir!"
[Give me a free
country or death.]

Augusto C. Sandino

From 1927 to 1933 Augusto C. Sandino's guerrilla fighters challenged the much larger and better-equipped force of U.S. Marines for control of Nicaragua. Sandino became a folk hero throughout Latin America and a symbol of pride, independence, and self-determination. Sandino's persistent campaign caused the United States to shift its foreign policy toward Nicaragua and other Central American nations from direct military involvement to more subtle forms of intervention.

In the 1960s and 1970s a new version of Sandino's war was played out in Nicaragua. Then the Sandinista Front for National Liberation (which took Sandino's name) fought the armed forces of U.S.-backed dictator Anastasio Somoza Debayle. In 1979 the Sandinistas were victorious.

Experiences hunger and plenty as a child

Sandino (pronounced san-DEE-no) was born in 1894 in the village of Niquinohomo (population one thousand), in the Central American country of Nicaragua. He was the son of a wealthy merchant named Gregorio Sandino and Sandino's

Indian servant Margarita Calderón. For the first eleven years of Augusto's life he was disregarded by his father. The young Augusto either stayed home alone or went out begging or stealing food while his mother worked on a coffee plantation. As soon as he was able to work, Augusto joined his mother in the fields.

At the age of nine, Augusto and his mother were thrown in jail for receiving advance pay at one plantation, then jumping at the chance for a better-paying job. While in the jail cell, Augusto's mother had a miscarriage and Augusto had to nurse her back to health. Augusto later described his childhood as one of sorrow and misery.

When Augusto was eleven years old, his father invited him to live in his house. There Augusto experienced an existence entirely different than the one he had known before. He no longer had to work and was able to attend school.

As a young man, Sandino learned business skills from his father. He then established his own produce company.

Flees country after violent dispute; develops radical politics

In 1921 Sandino became involved in a personal dispute and shot a man in the leg. As a result, Sandino was forced to leave his home. He went to La Ceiba in neighboring Honduras, where he worked as a mechanic and warehouseman at a sugar plantation. After a few months he left that post and traveled through Guatemala and Mexico, working at a variety of jobs as he went.

In 1923 Sandino found work in the oil industry in Tampico, Mexico. There he encountered U.S. businessmen, as well as Mexicans opposed to U.S. companies' exploitation of Mexico's natural resources. Sandino associated with Mexican nationalists (advocates of national independence) and members of the Industrial Workers of the World (IWW—a radical labor organization that flourished in the early 1900s and sought to form an international union of all the world's workers).

Through his Mexican comrades, Sandino also came to identify with his indigenous heritage and with the struggles of indigenous peoples throughout Latin America (Indians formed

American Interests in Nicaragua

American foreign policy toward Nicaragua in the early twentieth century was guided by the "Roosevelt Corollary" (1904). This statement by President Theodore Roosevelt (1858–1919; president from 1901–09)—an addendum to the earlier "Monroe Doctrine" (1823) prohibiting future European colonies in the Americas—explained that the United States, as a "civilized nation," may have to intervene in the affairs of other nations in the Americas to preserve the peace. The United States, however, selectively employed the Roosevelt Corollary in instances where U.S. financial interests were at stake.

At the turn of the century the United States supported a rebellion in Nicaragua against a president who opposed U.S. interests. Then in 1912 U.S. Marines were sent into Nicaragua to bolster a pro-American president and to protect the property of U.S. mining corporations and the banana-and-coffee-growing giant United Fruit Company. The marines remained in Nicaragua through 1933, except for a pullout in 1925–26. From 1927 to 1933 Sandino tried to seize control of his country from the marines and the wealthy industrialists they represented.

The marines were only withdrawn from Nicaragua after a pro-U.S. president, backed by Anastasio Somoza Garcia—chief

the majority of the population in Latin America yet lived as virtual slaves in the economy dominated by people of European heritage). He began to view American imperialism (the policy of establishing dominance over other nations)—and the export of profits from Nicaraguan natural resources and cheap labor—as the reason for Nicaragua's widespread poverty.

Organizes workers into rebel force

In 1926 Sandino returned to Nicaragua and took a job in an American-owned gold mine. There he talked with workers about the injustice of a foreign company extracting profits from Nicaragua and rallied the workers to fight for better pay and working conditions. Sandino explained that the government of the ruling Conservative Party defended only the interests of the rich.

Anastasio Somoza. *Reproduced by permission of Corbis Corporation (Bellevue).*

of Nicaragua's National Guard—had been installed. Two years after the marines pulled out, Somoza took power by force. The U.S.-backed Somoza (and later his sons) and the U.S.-trained National Guard ruled Nicaragua with an iron fist until they were overthrown by a popular revolt (by guerrilla fighters called Sandinistas; see box "Sandinos Spirit Resurrected in Sandinistas) in 1979. The Somozas, at the time they were deposed, owned half of the industrial and agricultural assets in Nicaragua and were worth hundreds of millions of dollars. As the Somozas had increased their personal wealth, the vast majority of Nicaraguans had sunk deeper into poverty.

Sandino gained a following among the workers. That October he convinced twenty-nine workers to join him in an armed battle to overthrow the government. Sandino turned to Liberal Party leader Juan B. Sacasa for support. (The Liberals and the Conservatives were the two major political parties in Nicaragua at the time.) Sacasa, who had been ousted from the presidency in an election tainted by fraud, had set up a provisional government on Nicaragua's east coast. He formed a loose association with Sandino (he did not agree with Sandino's tirades against owners and bosses), for the common purpose of overthrowing the ruling Conservatives.

In late 1926 and early 1927, with arms provided by the Liberal Party leaders, Sandino's forces (which had grown to one hundred men) twice occupied the northern town of Jinotega. In response, the U.S. government, which had recalled marines from Nicaragua, sent two thousand marines back to that nation.

Sandino's association with the Liberals ended in May 1927, when the Liberals agreed to a compromise with the Conservative Party and the American government. The Liberals accepted an offer to control a portion of the country and the promise of U.S.-monitored elections. Sandino and his men, in contrast, were unconvinced that the deal would change the power relationship and prepared to battle the marines. They set up a base in the northern town of San Rafael del Norte. On May 18, 1927, Sandino married a telegraph worker named Blanca Arauz.

Conducts guerrilla war against U.S. Marines

Sandino launched his first offensive against a marine garrison on July 16, 1927, in Ocotal. Sandino's attack surprised the marines and would likely have been victorious if U.S. warplanes had not flown in and defended the installation. The battle, however, drew international attention to the Nicaraguan conflict.

Sandino remained steadfast in his fight for national sovereignty. "I prefer to lose your love and die in battle," Sandino wrote to his wife in October 1927, "than to . . . survive in . . . oppression. I place above all loves the love of my country." Sandino compared himself to American revolutionary leader George Washington (1732–1799; president 1789–97) in that both had struggled for the liberty of their people. He blamed the greed of foreign interests and wealthy Nicaraguans for his people's social ills.

After the Ocotal battle, Sandino changed his strategy from direct attacks to hit-and-run assaults on specific targets and ambushes on the rear flanks of advancing marine units. He had great success with that method; his forces inflicted substantial damage upon a much larger and more well-equipped enemy. Sandino sustained his guerrilla war for five years. In 1931 Sandino targeted U.S. business interests, taking over the headquarters of American logging companies and facilities of the United Fruit Company.

Marines leave Nicaragua; agreement reached

Although Sandino was a hunted man in Nicaragua, he won many supporters in the United States and throughout

Sandino's Spirit Resurrected in Sandinistas

In 1961 the fighting spirit of Sandino was resurrected in a new rebel army—comprised of students, workers, and peasants—called the Sandinista Front for National Liberation (known by the Spanish acronym FSLN, or Sandinistas). The Sandinistas gained widespread support among the Nicaraguan people and toppled the U.S.-backed Somoza dictatorship on July 19, 1979. Among the ranks of the Sandinista fighters were two of Sandino's grandsons.

Upon taking power, the Sandinistas nationalized land and major industries. They created farming cooperatives on which landless peasants could work together to raise crops. They undertook massive literacy and vaccination drives. The Sandinista experiment, however, was not given much of a chance to work. In 1980 the U.S. government established and armed a rebel group known as the "Contras." The Contras attacked civilians and burned down cooperatives, schools, and health centers. The Contra war forced the Sandinistas to divert precious resources to national defense. The Sandinistas also had to institute an unpopular draft. As a result of the war, the death toll rose to over thirty thousand, and the economy faltered.

The U.S. government agreed to stop funding the Contras in exchange for free elections in Nicaragua to be held in 1990. Some $20 million was pumped into an opposition coalition's campaign by the U.S. Congress and the Central Intelligence Agency (CIA). On February 25, 1990, the Sandinistas lost the elections to the U.S.-backed group National Opposition Union (known by the Spanish acronym UNO).

Latin America. Eventually the U.S. government came to question the policy of military intervention in Nicaragua. In January 1933 the marines were pulled out of Nicaragua. They left in their place the Nicaraguan National Guard—a force armed and trained by the marines.

Sandino then entered into negotiations with Juan B. Sacasa, who had been elected Nicaraguan president. Sandino agreed to stop fighting in exchange for amnesty for him and his men, land for an agricultural cooperative, and the retention of an army of a hundred troops for one year. Sandino formed an organization called the Autonomist Party and prepared to enter the political process.

On June 2, 1933, Sandino faced a personal tragedy when his wife died in childbirth. At the same time, however, he gained a daughter whom he named Blanca Segovia.

Assassinated by Somoza

Even after the truce went into effect, Sandino's supporters faced harassment from the National Guard. Sandino himself was the target of a personal grudge by National Guard Chief Anastasio Somoza Garcia.

On February 21, 1934, Sandino accepted an invitation to dine with President Sacasa. After dinner Sandino and two of his generals were detained in their car by National Guardsmen. They were driven to an airfield in the capital city, Managua, and executed.

Somoza claimed credit for the killing. Two years later Somoza forcibly took over the presidency. The Somoza family, and their feared National Guard, relentlessly ruled Nicaragua from 1937 to 1979.

Sources

Books

"Augusto César Sandino." *Dictionary of Hispanic Biography*. Detroit: Gale Research, Inc., 1996.

Cabezas, Omar. *Fire from the Mountain: The Making of a Sandinista*. New York: Crown Publishers, Inc., 1985.

Macauly, Neill. *The Sandino Affair*. Chicago: Quadrangle Books, 1967.

Walker, Thomas W. *Nicaragua: The Land of Sandino*. 2nd ed. Boulder, CO: Westview Press, 1986.

Articles

Gaynor, Tim, and Duncan Campbell. "Freedom Fighter's Daughter Keeps Faith." *The Guardian* (London). June 29, 1999: 11.

"Decade of Conflict: A Look at Sandinista Rule." *Boston Globe*. February 27, 1990: 6.

O'Brien, Conor Cruise. "God and Man in Nicaragua." *The Atlantic*. August 1986: 50+.

Rose, Jonathan. "The War-Torn Roots of Today's Turmoil; Civil Wars Have Plagued Central American Nations for More than 160 years." *Scholastic Update*. March 9, 1987: 19+.

Mario Savio

Born December 8, 1942
New York City
Died November 6, 1996
Sebastopol, California

Free speech activist, civil rights activist, and educator

From the 1960s through the 1990s Mario Savio fought for political freedoms, the rights of minority groups and poor people, and peace. As the eloquent leader of the 1964 Free Speech Movement at the University of California-Berkeley, Savio challenged university regulations forbidding student political groups from spreading their messages on campus. He rallied hundreds of students to occupy a campus building and subject themselves to arrest. The Free Speech Movement is credited with having ushered in an era of antiwar protest and countercultural rebellion at colleges and universities around the United States.

Grows up in New York City

Savio was born on December 8, 1942, in Queens, New York, and grew up in a working-class neighborhood. His father, a native of Sicily, was a sheet-metal worker. Savio was a Catholic altar boy and attended Martin Van Buren High School. He graduated at the top of his class of 1,200 people. Savio then received a scholarship to the Catholic Manhattan College. After one year he transferred to Queens College.

"He symbolized the possibilities in all of us, to resist becoming cogs in somebody's machine."

Tom Hayden after hearing of Savio's death in 1996

Mario Savio.
Reproduced by permission of AP/Wide World Photos.

Early advocate of affirmative action

In the fall of 1963 Savio moved to California to attend the University of California-Berkeley (UC-Berkeley). He majored in philosophy and became involved in the civil rights movement. In March 1964 Savio and other activists were arrested at a demonstration at the Sheraton Palace, a hotel in San Francisco, California, protesting the hotel's refusal to hire African Americans for positions other than maids. The demonstrators were ultimately successful in forcing a change in the hiring policies of the San Francisco Hotel Association (of which the Sheraton Palace was a member).

As Savio stated in 1995, that 1964 protest was the beginning "of affirmative action before the name caught on." (Affirmative action is a set of federal government policies, adopted in the early 1970s, that provide increased educational and employment opportunities to racial minorities and women in order to overcome past patterns of discrimination.)

Participates in Freedom Summer

In the spring of 1964 Savio answered the call of the **Student Nonviolent Coordinating Committee** (SNCC; see entry) to participate in "Freedom Summer" in Mississippi. Freedom Summer was a massive voter-registration and desegregation campaign undertaken by approximately one thousand volunteers—most of them white students from northern and western colleges. Before Savio and the other volunteers headed south, they attended a week-long training session. There SNCC leaders warned participants about the dangers of doing civil rights work in Mississippi and schooled them in techniques of nonviolent action—how to defy authority but not strike back when attacked.

In late June 1964 Freedom Summer volunteers descended upon Mississippi. They conducted door-to-door voter-registration drives and established community centers, health clinics, legal clinics, and community feeding sites called "freedom kitchens." Savio was one of several volunteers teaching at "freedom schools" for African American children.

Savio and other Freedom Summer workers were well aware of the dangerous nature of their mission. Shortly before the volunteers arrived in Mississippi, they had received word that three advance-team members—James Chaney, Michael Schwerner, and Andrew Goodman—were missing. In late August the bodies of the trio were found near the town of Philadelphia, Mississippi. An investigation determined that they had been killed by members of the Ku Klux Klan (a white supremacist group).

UC-Berkeley clamps down on free speech

In the fall of 1964 Savio returned to campus and took over the reins of the Berkeley chapter of the Friends of SNCC. The goal of the organization was to raise funds and sign up volunteers for continuing civil rights work in Mississippi. That fall, however, UC-Berkeley administrators issued new regulations forbidding student organizations from engaging in political speech, raising funds, distributing literature, circulating petitions, or publicizing meetings on campus.

Savio could not quietly accept the new rules. "I spent the summer in Mississippi," Savio was quoted as saying in "Mario Savio, 53, Campus Protester, Dies," published in the *New York Times* after his death in 1996. "I witnessed tyranny. I saw groups of men in the minority working their wills over the majority. Then I came back here and found the university preventing us from collecting money for use there and even stopping us from getting people to go to Mississippi to help."

Birth of the Free Speech Movement

Savio worked with representatives of other student groups to form a coalition called the Free Speech Movement (FSM). The organizations in the FSM spanned the political spectrum from conservative to radical. The FSM charged that the administration's measures abridged students' constitutional rights to free expression. The FSM executive committee, of which Savio was a member, mapped out a strategy to challenge the rules.

The FSM got off to a fiery start in early October, when student activist Jack Weinberg was arrested for distributing civil rights literature. Savio jumped onto the roof of the police car in which Weinberg was being detained and beckoned other students to surround the car. Nearly three thousand students heeded the call. Savio grabbed the microphone from the police car and gave a speech over the loudspeaker. (A photograph of Savio on top of the car was carried in newspapers around the world). A string of student speeches from the car's rooftop followed, lasting thirty-two straight hours.

The students were eventually persuaded to abandon the car in favor of a meeting with administrators. University officials, however, refused to revoke the ban on political activity, and the protests continued.

Free Speech Movement gains steam

The climax of the Free Speech Movement came on December 2, 1964, when students took over Sproul Hall, the campus administration building. At a rally before the "sit-in," Savio spoke his now-famous words regarding the "knowledge factory" mentality of the university: "There comes a time when the operation of the machine becomes so odious, makes you so sick at heart, that you can't take part, you can't even passively take part. And you've got to put your bodies on the gears, and upon the wheels, upon the levers, upon all the apparatus, and you've got to make it stop. And you've got to indicate to the people who . . . own it, that unless you're free, the machine will be prevented from working at all!"

Savio and 782 others were arrested twenty-eight hours after the occupation began. That sit-in was the first major college protest of the era to receive national media coverage. Regarding the events of that date, Savio later stated, "For the first time, students used civil disobedience to get their own rights." For his role as a leader in the action, Savio was sentenced to four months in prison and was expelled from school.

Administration changes policy

The ideological gulf between university administrators and student activists could not have been wider. While students called for free expression, administrators likened the university to a "knowledge factory" and considered political activity a hindrance to productivity. Clark Kerr, University of California chancellor, held steadfast to the ban on political activity. He referred to the FSM as "a ritual of hackneyed complaints" and accused the group of being directed by communists. (Communists are people who embrace a type of social organization based on the holding of all property in common.)

Soon after the December 2 student action, however, Kerr found himself increasingly isolated in his unyielding position against the FSM's demands. He backed down under pressure from faculty members and other administrators. On December 8, the U-C Academic Senate passed a resolution granting students the right to engage in political activity on campus. Soon thereafter Kerr was fired.

Avoids spotlight in post-FSM period

After his expulsion from school, Savio stayed in Berkeley and worked as a bookstore clerk, a private math tutor, and a bartender. He shunned media interviews and tried to lose the trappings of celebrity that had been forced on him during the previous months. (Savio, who was an advocate of participatory democracy, hated being called a "leader.") Savio was arrested once more at UC-Berkeley in 1966, protesting armed forces recruitment on campus. (The antiarmed forces sentiment was largely due to the Vietnam War, 1954–75). That same year Savio launched an unsuccessful bid for U.S. Senate on the antiwar Peace and Freedom Party ticket.

Over the next several years Savio taught mathematics in public and private junior high schools and high schools. He married FSM leader Suzanne Goldberg; the couple had two children and later divorced. Savio's second marriage was to another former FSM activist, Lynne Hollander. Savio and Hollander had one child together.

Resumes education and teaching career

In the early 1980s Savio resumed his education at San Francisco State University. He completed a bachelor's degree in physics in 1984 and his master's degree a year later. In the late

FBI Places Savio under Surveillance

Savio's 1964 activities with the Free Speech Movement (FSM) came to the attention of the Federal Bureau of Investigation (FBI). The FBI added Savio to its list of political activists to be kept under surveillance.

Seth Rosenfeld, a reporter with the *San Francisco Examiner*, learned in 1995 that the FBI investigation of Savio had continued long after the FSM had met its goals and disbanded. Documents obtained by Rosenfeld under the Freedom of Information Act revealed that the FBI originally had been investigating Savio for ties with communists. Even after the FBI had concluded that Savio "had negligible contacts with Communists," they continued to spy on him due to his "contemptuous attitude."

1980s Savio taught at San Francisco State University and at Modesto Junior College. Throughout the 1980s Savio was active in the fights against apartheid (the legal system based on racial segregation and discrimination) in South Africa and against U.S. intervention in Nicaragua (see entry on **Augusto Cesar Sandino**).

In 1990 Savio began teaching mathematics and physics to remedial students at Sonoma State University in Rohnert Park, California—a position he held until his death. As a faculty member, Savio was active in the fight against increases in student fees. "He brought that same kind of enthusiasm that he had in the '60s to his teaching," stated colleague David Averbuck in a 1996 *New York Times* article about Savio, "and the students really appreciated it."

Attends thirtieth anniversary reunion of Free Speech protesters

Savio attended the thirtieth anniversary reunion of the Free Speech Movement in 1994. At the four-day event, Savio tried to persuade his fellow activists to take up social issues pertaining to economic justice.

At the time of the reunion, Savio was involved in the movement to prevent the passage of California's Proposition 187. That ballot initiative, which passed with 59 percent of the vote, ended government assistance (such as welfare, health care, and education) to undocumented workers and their children. The initiative has not been implemented because of legal challenges. Savio referred to Proposition 187 as a "know-nothing fascist law." (Fascism is a political system characterized by a dictator with complete power, the forcible suppression of opposition, and the promotion of nationalism and racism.)

Defends affirmative action in final days

Savio's final political battle was against a ballot initiative called Proposition 209. That initiative, which passed in 1996, ended the policy of affirmative action in California government agencies and pertained to employment, contracts, and admissions to publicly funded colleges and universities.

Savio (who had a history of heart problems) died of heart failure on November 6, 1996—on the eve of the passage of Proposition 209. He was fifty-three years old.

"In the '60s, he was a powerful symbol of how an ordinary person could stand up and make history," stated **Tom Hayden** (see entry)—another 1960s campus protester—upon hearing of Savio's death, as reported in the *San Francisco Examiner*. "He symbolized the possibilities in all of us, to resist becoming cogs in somebody's machine."

In December 1997 Savio was honored by UC-Berkeley—the school that had previously expelled him. A plaque was placed at the steps leading up to Sproul Hall, officially designating the area as the "Mario Savio Steps."

Sources

Books
Burns, Stewart. *Social Movements of the 1960s: Searching for Democracy.* Boston: Twayne Publishers, 1990.

Gitlin, Todd. *The Sixties: Years of Hope, Days of Rage.* New York: Bantam Books, 1987.

Articles
Hatfield, Larry D. "Mario Savio Dies; Free Speech Activist." *San Francisco Examiner.* November 7, 1996.

Jerome, Richard. "Radical Creak: 30th Anniversary of Free Speech Movement." *People Weekly.* December 19, 1994: 44+.

Kleffman, Sandy. "UC-Berkeley Changes Stance to Honor Free-Speech Movement Founder." Knight-Ridder/Tribune News Service. December 3, 1997.

Marcus, Greil. "Tributes: Mario Savio." *Rolling Stone.* December 26, 1996-January 9, 1997: 98+.

Pace, Eric. "Mario Savio, 53, Campus Protester, Dies." *New York Times.* November 7, 1996: D27.

Schechner, Mark. "Remembering Mario Savio." *Tikkun.* January-February 1997: 27+.

Web Sites
Barker, Karlyn. "Rebel with a Cause: Mario Savio, The Spark of the '60s College Protests." (Reprinted from Washington Post.) [Online] Available http://www.wenet.net/~anya/post.html (accessed March 14, 2000).

"Mario Savio on Free Speech." [Online] Available http://www.fsm-a.org/#Mario (accessed March 14, 2000).

Scheer, Robert. "The Man Who Stopped the Machine." (Reprinted from Los Angeles Times.) [Online] Available http://www.wenet.net/~anya/sheer.html (accessed March 14, 2000).

Fred Shuttlesworth

Born March 18, 1922
Mount Meigs, Alabama

Civil rights activist and minister

Fred Shuttlesworth.
*Reproduced by permission of
AP/Wide World Photos.*

Fred Shuttlesworth is a veteran of the war for civil rights in America. Like veterans of other wars, he has the scars to prove it. While fighting for desegregation, voting rights, and equal employment opportunities in the 1950s and 1960s, Shuttlesworth's home was bombed three times, he was arrested more than thirty times, beaten dozens of times by thugs—some of them from the Ku Klux Klan (a white supremacist group—sometimes with iron pipes and baseball bats. One time he was blasted unconscious by a high-powered water hose. At the end of the twentieth century, when most other civil rights leaders had died or faded into obscurity, Shuttlesworth remained on the front lines for change.

Youth and education

Freddie Lee Robinson was born on March 18, 1922, in Mount Meigs (Montgomery County), Alabama. At the age of three he moved with his mother, Alberta Robinson, his father Vedder Greene, and his baby sister to the town of Oxmoor, in Jefferson County, Alabama. In 1927 Fred's mother (who was never married to Vedder Greene) married

William Nathan Shuttlesworth. Fred and his sister took their stepfather's name.

Shuttlesworth graduated from Rosedale High School in 1940. The next year he married Ruby Lanette Keeler, from Birmingham, Alabama. The couple eventually had four children (Patricia, Ruby, Fred, Jr., and Carolyn). The marriage ended in divorce in 1970.

Trains to be a minister

In 1943, the year that his first child was born, Shuttlesworth began attending Cedar Grove Academy Bible College in Pritchard, Alabama. He also began preaching at a Baptist church. Shuttlesworth supported his family by working at an air force base as a truck driver.

In 1947 Shuttlesworth continued his education at Selma University in Selma, Alabama. The next year he was ordained a Baptist minister. In 1949 Shuttlesworth moved his family to Montgomery, Alabama, so he could attend Alabama State College and serve as pastor of the First (African) Baptist Church. Three years later Shuttlesworth quit that position after a dispute with church leaders and moved to Birmingham. There he took over the reigns of the Bethel Baptist Church in Collegeville, North Birmingham.

Begins civil rights activism

Shuttlesworth began his involvement with civil rights activism in July 1955, when he called on the Birmingham City Commission to hire African American police officers. Shuttlesworth's petition, which was signed by seventy-six African American ministers, was ignored. Shuttlesworth then led a delegation to city hall to press the issue, but his plea again fell on deaf ears.

That December Shuttlesworth turned his attention to the matter of racial discrimination on city buses (as in most other locations in the American South, in Birmingham African Americans had to sit in the rear of the bus). Shuttlesworth heard about the start of the Montgomery bus boycott (the refusal of African Americans to ride city buses in protest of the racist seating policy; see entry on **Jo Ann Gibson Robinson**), and began attending meetings of the Montgomery Improve-

Shuttlesworth leaving Graymont Elementary School with the Armstrong brothers after they were denied admittance.

Reproduced by permission of Corbis Corporation (Bellevue).

ment Association (MIA)—the organization coordinating the boycott. The following year he led a smaller-scale bus campaign in Birmingham, in which he and others purposely disobeyed the segregation rules on buses on appointed days.

Founds Alabama Christian Movement for Human Rights

In June 1956 a circuit court judge outlawed all activities of the National Association for the Advancement of Colored People (NAACP) in Alabama. In response, Shuttlesworth organized a new civil rights organization: the Alabama Christian Movement for Human Rights (ACMHR). Like the NAACP, the ACMHR was dedicated to dismantling segregation (legally mandated separation of the races). From 1956 to 1966 Shuttlesworth served as the group's president.

In February 1957, following the victory of the Montgomery bus boycott (Montgomery buses were desegregated by court order), Shuttlesworth traveled to Atlanta, Georgia, for the founding of the Southern Christian Leadership Conference (SCLC). The SCLC was established as an organization of African American ministers to coordinate civil rights activities in the South. The group elected **Martin Luther King, Jr.** (1929–1968; see entry), as its first president. That August Shuttlesworth became the group's secretary. In that capacity he became a close aide to and confidant of King. The SCLC quickly rose to prominence as the South's most respected civil rights organization.

Later that year Shuttlesworth led a campaign to desegregate Birmingham's public schools. As part of that effort, he attempted to enroll his daughters Pat and Ruby at the city's all-white high school. For that action Shuttlesworth was beaten by a group of whites—some using baseball bats and bicycle chains. Shuttlesworth suffered a concussion, and his wife and one daughter sustained slight injuries. Shuttlesworth's activism in 1957 won him the title "Newsmaker of the Year" by the publication *Birmingham World.*

Aids wounded Freedom Riders

Shuttlesworth watched with anticipation as an integrated group of thirteen civil rights activists began the Freedom Rides on May 4, 1961. The Freedom Rides, organized by the nonviolent activist group Congress on Racial Equality (CORE), involved the attempts by black and white riders to ride together on interstate (crossing state lines) buses throughout the South. The purpose of the Freedom Rides was to test the Supreme Court's rulings ordering the desegregation of interstate buses and transportation facilities.

One of the worst cases of violence against the Freedom Riders occurred in Anniston, Alabama—sixty-six miles east of Birmingham—on May 14 (Mother's Day). As the Greyhound bus drove through Anniston, it was set upon by a mob of whites. The attackers smashed the bus's windows with iron bars, tire chains, and clubs, and slashed its tires. As the bus pulled away from the station, it was pursued by carloads of assailants. Shuttlesworth received a call about the attack on the bus and quickly organized a caravan to provide aid to the riders.

Birmingham in the Pre-Civil Rights Era

Birmingham, Alabama, the place Shuttlesworth called home, was one of the most hostile places toward African Americans in the South in the pre-civil rights years. In a 1963 article in the *Pittsburgh Courier,* an African American weekly newspaper, African American leaders labeled Birmingham the "worst big city in the U.S.A." And according to Martin Luther King, Jr., Birmingham was "probably the most thoroughly segregated city in the United States."

Prior to May 1963, virtually every public facility in Birmingham was racially segregated—down to its ball parks, taxicabs, and libraries. In 1962, rather than complying with a federal desegregation order, the city had opted to close sixty-eight parks, thirty-eight playgrounds, six swimming pools, and four golf courses.

Antiblack violence in the city at the time was widespread. Harrison Salisbury, a reporter for the *New York Times,* wrote that in Birmingham, the "emotional dynamite of racism [was] reinforced by the whip, the razor, the gun, the bomb, the torch, the club, the knife, the mob, the police and many branches of the state's apparatus." Between 1957 and 1963 there were eighteen "unsolved" (for lack of investigation) bombings in Birmingham's African American neighborhoods. For this reason the city was nicknamed "Bombingham"; an African American neighborhood that was hit particularly hard was called "Dynamite Hill." Shuttlesworth's own church, the Bethel Baptist Church (to which his home was attached), was bombed three times.

Six miles outside of Anniston, the bus had a flat tire and was forced to stop at a service station. The mob caught up to the bus and swarmed around it. One person threw a fire-bomb through the rear door of the bus and jammed the door shut. The bus's occupants managed to escape just before the bus burst into flames. Once outside the bus, the freedom riders were beaten by the crowd.

Shuttlesworth and his colleagues arrived on the scene just in time to load the wounded riders into cars and drive them to Birmingham. Shuttlesworth's courageous act is credited with having saved the lives of the freedom riders on that day.

Draws King to Birmingham for desegregation campaign

In late 1962 Shuttlesworth led an african American boycott of white merchants in an attempt to desegregate downtown Birmingham. Protesters in front of stores, however, were brutally attacked by police and their dogs. Shuttlesworth was one of more than forty protesters arrested during the campaign. He became convinced that the only way victory could be achieved in Birmingham was with outside help.

In early 1963 Shuttlesworth persuaded the SCLC to make Birmingham its next target for desegregation. Shuttlesworth argued that Birmingham should be chosen because it was the most segregated city in the South (see box about Birmingham). In addition, Shuttlesworth noted that Birmingham was home to a vicious police chief named Eugene "Bull" Connor. As civil rights activists had learned in other places, a successful campaign required more than just a setting of pervasive racial injustice. It also called for a display of brutality on the part of white mobs and the police against peaceful African American demonstrators. Shuttlesworth correctly predicted that Connor would display the violence necessary to capture the attention of the national press and thereby begin the process of dismantling the city's system of segregation.

Puts "Project C" in motion

In January 1963 Shuttlesworth met with SCLC leaders King, Ralph Abernathy (1926–1990; who became SCLC president upon King's death in 1968), and Wyatt Walker (1929–) to map out a careful course of action called "Project C" (the "C" stood for Confrontation). The plan included boycotts of selected downtown department stores (those that had segregated lunch counters or otherwise discriminated against African Americans), sit-ins, marches, and other demonstrations that would invariably lead to arrest.

On Wednesday, April 3, 1963, King and the other SCLC leaders arrived in Birmingham. They presented city officials with a list of demands including the desegregation of downtown lunch counters, stores, and restrooms, and an end to discrimination in employment. The organizers' petition was ignored.

April 3 marked the beginning of four days of sit-ins at segregated lunch counters in department stores and drugstores. Shuttlesworth personally led marches on city hall. Those actions resulted in the arrest of more than 180 protesters. On the fifth day of demonstrations, officers used nightsticks and snarling dogs to attack members of a prayer procession. The melee was captured on television, and the nation's attention turned to Birmingham.

Children take to the streets

As "Project C" entered its third week, the jails filled up and the ranks of adult protesters thinned. As a result, SCLC staffers began recruiting high-school students for the campaign.

The first youth march was held on May 2, 1963. More than one thousand African American children, from six to eighteen years of age, gathered at the Sixteenth Street Baptist Church and listened to a speech by King. Then they filed out of the church and into the street, where they sang freedom songs and knelt in prayer. Nine-hundred-fifty-nine children were arrested that day.

Brutality against children shocks the world

The next day a thousand students again gathered inside the Sixteenth Street Baptist Church. That time, however, Bull Connor was determined to stop the "Children's Crusade." He ordered firefighters and dogs to the scene and instructed his police force to block all church entrances.

While about half of the children remained trapped inside the church, the other half escaped and ran across the street to a park. To the shock of people throughout the United States, who were watching the incident on television, all forms of brutality were unleashed on the fleeing youngsters. The children were clubbed by police, chased and attacked by dogs, and assaulted with a new weapon: the firehose.

On orders of Connor, firefighters set their hoses to one hundred pounds per square inch—a pressure great enough to rip the bark from a tree. Turned on the protesters, the water tore people's clothing, cut their skin, slammed them into parked cars, knocked them to the ground, and rolled them down the street.

Shuttlesworth, who was attempting to help children, was himself blasted by a firehose. He was knocked unconscious, suffered a broken rib, and was hospitalized. "I caught sight of the powerful stream of water arching down upon me less than fifty feet away," Shuttlesworth told a reporter from *Ebony* magazine. "Quickly I put my hands over my face and turned away as the wind was knocked out of me, my chest ached, my head pounded, and my heart was trying to burst. Had I not thrown up my hands, my face probably would have been disfigured."

In a 1993 interview Shuttlesworth reminisced about the Children's Crusade. "The kids were marvelous soldiers," Shuttlesworth stated. "I think the greatest soldiers that have ever been in this country are the civil rights soldiers of 1956 to 1963 and especially the children."

Desegregation accord reached

Fueled by anger at the treatment of the children, thousands of people demonstrated over the next few days. Some brandished bottles, bricks, guns, and knives. As the crowd of protesters surged, the police, attack dogs, and firefighters attempted to confine them to the African American part of town. Between May 4 and May 6, more than two thousand demonstrators were arrested.

The month of sustained protests finally brought Birmingham merchants and lawmakers to the table. On May 10, 1963, an accord was reached that promised an end to segregation of downtown stores (including lunch counters, restrooms, fitting rooms, and drinking fountains) and the hiring of African Americans in clerical and sales positions.

Moves to Cincinnati

Beginning in 1961, Shuttlesworth spent part of his time in Cincinnati, Ohio, where he served as pastor of the Revelation Baptist Church. Civil rights activities in the South, however, still commanded much of his time through the end of 1963.

In late 1965 Shuttlesworth came under attack by some Revelation Baptist Church members for what they felt was his dictatorial style and a misuse of church funds. Although an audit cleared Shuttlesworth of the second charge, feelings of ill will between him and some parishioners remained. In 1966, with 150 of his supporters from the Revelation Baptist Church,

Shuttlesworth founded a new church in Cincinnati: the Greater New Light Baptist Church.

In the three-plus decades since the Birmingham accords, Shuttlesworth has been involved in a variety of civil rights issues—from the integration of beaches in St. Augustine, Florida, to promoting voting rights in Selma, Alabama, to the institution of fair employment practices at a hospital in Cincinnati. In 1992 an eight-foot-tall statue of Shuttlesworth was erected in front of the Birmingham Civil Rights Institute and Museum.

As the 1990s came to a close, Shuttlesworth could still be found in the pulpit of the Greater New Light Baptist Church and at civil rights demonstrations around the United States.

"I don't want people to look at me as some great historical [figure]," Shuttlesworth stated in a 1999 news article. "I'm just like you, but God has put something in me. He's put something in you, too."

Sources

Books

Manis, Andrew M. *A Fire You Can't Put Out: The Civil Rights Life of Birmingham's Reverend Fred Shuttlesworth.* Tuscaloosa: University of Alabama Press, 1999.

Powledge, Fred. *Free At Last? The Civil Rights Movement and the People Who Made It.* Boston: Little, Brown and Company, 1991.

"Shuttlesworth, Fred L." *The African American Encyclopedia.* Vol. 5. Edited by Michael W. Williams. New York: Marshall Cavendish, 1993.

White, Marjorie L. *A Walk to Freedom: The Reverend Fred Shuttlesworth and the Alabama Christian Movement for Human Rights, 1956–1964.* Birmingham: Birmingham Historical Society, 1998.

Articles

Bearden, Michelle. "It's All about Justice." *Tampa Tribune.* September 7, 1999: 1.

Galloway, Angela. "A Civil Rights Legend Presses on in Chesco." *The Inquirer* (Philadelphia). February 1, 1999.

Yardley, Jim. "That Bomb Took All the Fear from Me." *Atlanta Journal and Constitution.* August 28, 1993: A2.

Web Sites

"Wasn't That a Time?" Center for Civil Rights. [Online] Available http://hrcr.law.columbia.edu/ccr/index.html (accessed March 7, 2000).

Elizabeth Cady Stanton

Born November 12, 1815
Johnstown, New York
Died October 26, 1902
New York, New York

Women's rights activist, feminist philosopher, and writer

Elizabeth Cady Stanton was a visionary leader of the women's rights movement of the nineteenth century. While raising seven children, Stanton distinguished herself as a writer, speaker, philosopher, and political organizer. At a time when women were supposed to live in the shadows of their husbands or fathers, Stanton took very public stands for women's voting rights, the right of women to obtain divorces, women's property rights, temperance (the banning of alcohol), birth control, and dress reform. Stanton was a cofounder of the 1848 Seneca Falls convention for women's rights—a gathering that ushered in the modern women's rights movement. Stanton was ahead of her time in calling for full equality between the sexes in all aspects of life.

Educated at boys' school

Stanton was born in 1815 and raised in Johnstown, New York. Her father, Daniel Cady, was a respected lawyer who became a judge on the New York Supreme Court. As a child, Stanton attended Johnstown Academy—a boys' school—where she excelled in debate and language studies. Since

"Come, come, my conservative friend. Wipe the dew off your spectacles and see that the world is moving."

Elizabeth Cady Stanton, The Woman's Bible, *1895*

Elizabeth Cady Stanton.
National Archives and Records Administration.

515

women were not allowed to enroll in colleges in the early nineteenth century, Stanton attended Emma Willard's Troy Female Seminary in Troy, New York. There she studied logic, science, and political science.

After graduating in 1833 Stanton spent her days in her father's law office, studying legal and constitutional history. She expressed outrage at laws that discriminated against women and vowed to change them. Stanton's father found his daughter's interests "inappropriate" for a young woman and attempted to steer Stanton in the direction of becoming a wife and mother. "To think all in me," Stanton wrote in 1855, "of which my father would have felt a proper pride had I been a man is deeply mortifying to him because I am a woman."

Stanton grew up during a time when women were regarded as physically and intellectually inferior to men. Valued mainly for their ability to bear children, women were considered the property of, or extensions of, their husbands or fathers. Women did not have the right to own property, to vote, or to use birth control. A woman's earnings legally belonged to her father, guardian, or husband. Stanton belonged to a generation of women who began to voice their grievances and call for change.

Marries an abolitionist

In 1840 Stanton, against the wishes of her conservative family, married the abolitionist (one who works for an end to slavery) Henry B. Stanton (1805–1887). Henry Stanton was an organizer, speaker, writer, and politician. In a move considered radical at the time, Stanton kept her birth name, Cady, as part of her married name.

The Stantons eventually had seven children. Stanton managed to combine her household and child-rearing duties with her work in the women's rights movement.

Organizes the Seneca Falls convention

Stanton and her close friend, Quaker abolitionist Lucretia Mott (1793–1880), frequently discussed the political and social status of women in the United States. In 1848 Stanton, Mott, and several other women decided to call a public meeting to discuss women's rights—particularly property rights, voting rights, the right to enroll in institutions of higher learning, and the right to receive pay equal to that of men for equal work. More than three hundred people (among them forty men) attended the two-day convention held in Seneca Falls, New York. During the meeting Stanton read her famous "Declaration of Sentiments" speech (see box), in which she proposed twelve resolutions for discussion and adoption.

A second convention was held two weeks later in Rochester, New York, where Stanton's "Declaration" was approved by a majority of the attendees. Stanton became a recognized leader of the women's rights movement. She then helped women throughout the country prepare for their own meetings and assemblies, thus sowing the seeds of a nationwide suffrage movement.

Works for women's property rights

In the early 1850s Stanton and her friend Susan B. Anthony (1820–1906; see box) threw their energies behind the women's property rights movement. With the help of sixty volunteers, the women collected six thousand signatures on a petition calling for women to have control over their belongings and children. Stanton and Anthony then took the petition to the state legislature in Albany, New York, where they gave moving appeals. Not surprisingly, the all-male legislature rejected the idea of a property-rights law.

Stanton and Anthony continued their efforts. While Stanton, homebound with six children, could do little more

Declaration of Sentiments

What follows is an excerpt from Stanton's "Declaration of Sentiments," the landmark speech she delivered at the 1848 Seneca Falls Women's convention.

. . . The history of mankind is a history of repeated injuries and usurpations on the part of man toward woman, having in direct object the establishment of an absolute tyranny over her. To prove this, let facts be submitted to a candid world.

He has never permitted her to exercise her inalienable right to elective franchise [the right to vote].

He has compelled her to submit to laws, in the formation of which she had no voice.

He has withheld from her rights which are given to the most ignorant and degraded men—both natives and foreigners.

Having deprived her of this first right of a citizen, the elective franchise, thereby leaving her without representation in the halls of legislation, he has oppressed her on all sides.

He has made her, if married, in the eye of the law, civilly dead.

He has taken from her all right in property, even to the wages she earns. . . .

Stanton's Partnership with Susan B. Anthony

In 1851 Stanton met fellow women's rights crusader Susan B. Anthony (1820–1906) while campaigning for temperance (the prohibition of the sale and use of alcohol). Both Stanton and Anthony were motivated to ban alcohol by a desire to stop the beatings of wives at the hands of drunken husbands. In that era there were no laws protecting women from spousal abuse.

In April 1852, Anthony—a Quaker and former teacher—enlisted the help of Stanton in organizing a women's temperance convention in New York. (The Sons of Temperance—the primary organization of the temperance movement at the time—did not allow women to participate in decision-making.) The New York meeting attracted five hundred women and initiated the founding of the Women's State Temperance Society. Stanton was elected the group's first president, and Anthony its first secretary.

The following year Stanton was ousted from the presidency by conservative members of the organization who disapproved of Stanton's call for the right of women to divorce drunken and abusive husbands. Anthony resigned in protest. Thereafter Stanton and Anthony devoted their energies to other aspects of the women's movement—primarily women's property rights and woman suffrage.

than compose speeches and offer encouragement, Anthony traveled the state collecting petition signatures. Finally, in 1860, after six years of campaigning, the women's hard work was rewarded with the passage of the Married Woman's Property Act. This legislation gave women control over their wages, property, and inheritances. The act also stated that "every married woman shall be joint guardian of her children with her husband, with equal powers regarding them." Soon thereafter the legislatures of many other states passed similar laws.

Lobbies for universal suffrage in post-Civil War era

Throughout the Civil War (1861–65), Stanton and Anthony had pushed for a constitutional amendment guaranteeing the freedom of slaves in every state. (The Emancipation

Susan B. Anthony. *Courtesy of the Library of Congress.*

The duo became one of the most dynamic and long-lasting partnerships for social change in the history of the United States. Stanton was the deep thinker and master strategist of the pair; Anthony was the great organizer. Anthony (who was free to travel because she was unmarried and had no children) put the ideas of Stanton (who was homebound with children) into action. Stanton wrote speeches and Anthony delivered them; Stanton wrote petitions and Anthony circulated them; Stanton planned conferences and Anthony worked out the logistics to make them happen. The two worked together for their cause for fifty years.

Proclamation, issued in 1863, only granted freedom to slaves in states at war with the Union [northern states], but not to slaves in border states [such as Missouri and West Virginia] within the Union.) The women's goal was achieved in 1864, when Congress passed the Thirteenth Amendment abolishing slavery.

In the post–Civil War period, Stanton and Anthony chose to dedicate their energy to securing voting rights for *all* Americans. Despite their efforts and those of countless other volunteers, the post-war amendments guaranteeing rights to African Americans did not enfranchise (give the vote to) women. The Fourteenth Amendment, ratified in 1868, granted all citizens equal protection under the law (meaning that all people, but interpreted as "all males," were to enjoy the same legal rights and protections). And the Fifteenth Amendment, ratified in 1870, granted all citizens, regardless of race or color, the right to vote (that right, however, would be revoked for African Americans by a series of racist laws before the turn of the twentieth century). In 1869 Anthony persuaded one lawmaker to introduce a women's suffrage bill into the U.S. House of Representatives, but it failed. That bill was reintroduced every year until its passage in 1920.

Founds National Woman Suffrage Association

In 1869 a split occurred within the women's movement, with one camp calling for immediate women's suffrage and the other camp applauding the right of African American males to vote (as provided by the Fifteenth Amendment) and advising patience in the matter of women's suffrage.

In May 1869 Stanton and Anthony founded the National Woman Suffrage Association (NWSA). The NWSA, with members from nineteen states, had as its goal the passage of a constitutional amendment granting women the right to vote. At the time, the NWSA was considered a radical organization: it did not admit men and even criticized the churches for their sexist teachings. Stanton was elected as the NSWA's first president. She served in that capacity until 1890.

The American Woman Suffrage Association (AWSA)—created in November 1869—differed from the NWSA in its more moderate stance. The AWSA was led by noted orator Lucy Stone (1818–1893; see box in **Alice Paul** entry) and author Julia Ward Howe (1819–1910). They selected a prominent minister, Henry Ward Beecher (1813–1887), as their president. Rather than push for a constitutional amendment, the AWSA opted to campaign for women's suffrage one state at a time.

Writes *History of Woman Suffrage* and *Woman's Bible*

In 1880 Stanton and Anthony joined forces with another woman, Matilda Jocelyn Gage, to begin collaboration on a book documenting the women's suffrage movement. They collected reminiscences and news clips from dozens of women activists. The first volume of *History of Woman Suffrage* was published in 1881 to tremendous critical acclaim. The trio published their second volume in 1882 and their third volume in 1886.

Stanton, in her old age, grew increasingly angered by the antiwoman bias she perceived in organized religion. Stanton's final book, *Woman's Bible,* was her attempt to reframe religion as a source of inspiration for women. She presented a feminist analysis of the Old Testament in two volumes that were published in 1895 and 1898, respectively.

Organizations merge to form National American Woman Suffrage Association

In 1890 the NWSA and AWSA put aside their differences and merged to form the National American Woman Suffrage Association (NAWSA). Stanton, then seventy-five years old, was elected the group's first president; Anthony, who was seventy years old in 1890, succeeded her two years later. NAWSA sponsored numerous demonstrations in support of a women's suffrage amendment in front of the White House and at other locations around the country.

It was not until 1919—seventeen years after Stanton's death—that the women's suffrage bill was approved by Congress. The following year it won ratification from the necessary thirty-six states (ratification by three-fourths of all states is necessary for the adoption of any constitutional amendment). The Nineteenth Amendment, adopted in 1920, guaranteed women the right to vote.

Philosophically ahead of her time

By the time of Stanton's death in 1902, she had fallen out of favor with many in the women's movement. Stanton's ideas of equality between the sexes were considered too extreme. While the mainstream of the women's movement was content to focus on the issue of suffrage, Stanton believed that a fundamental change in relations between the sexes was necessary. She challenged the commonly accepted division of labor in families, in which child-rearing was considered the sole domain of women. She questioned marriage itself—an institution that bound women even to abusive husbands—and supported liberal divorce laws. Stanton argued that women should be given every opportunity to fully develop and use their intellect.

It was not until the late 1960s that feminists embraced Stanton's ideals of sexual equality. Stanton is considered by the modern-day women's rights movement to be the philosophical mother of American feminism.

Sources

Books

Banner, Lois W. *Elizabeth Cady Stanton: A Radical for Woman's Rights*. Boston: Little, Brown and Company, 1980.

McElroy, Lorie Jenkins. *Women's Voices: A Documentary History of Women in America*. Vol. 1. Farmington Hills, MI: U•X•L, 1999, pp. 57–67.

Oakley, Mary Ann B. *Elizabeth Cady Stanton*. Old Westbury, NY: The Feminist Press, 1972.

Stanton, Elizabeth Cady. *The Woman's Bible*. 2 Vols. New York: European Publishing Company, 1895–1898.

Articles

Leuchtag, Alice. "Elizabeth Cady Stanton: Freethinker and Radical Revisionist." *The Humanist*. September-October 1996: 29+.

Newman, James L. "Becoming the Birthplace of Women's Rights: The Transformation of Seneca Falls, New York." *Focus*. Fall 1992: 4+.

Ruether, Rosemary Radford. "Fight for Women's Vote Key to Nation's Identity." *National Catholic Reporter*. November 15, 1996: 22.

Student Nonviolent Coordinating Committee

Founded 1960
Raleigh, North Carolina
Disbanded 1967

Student civil rights organization

The Student Nonviolent Coordinating Committee (SNCC; pronounced "snick") was an alliance of student civil rights activists who used direct-action tactics as a means of achieving racial equality on all levels of society. SNCC members worked throughout the South, encouraging ordinary people to participate in campaigns for desegregation and voter registration. Born out of the lunch-counter sit-in movement, SNCC positioned itself on the front lines of what amounted to a civil war over civil rights. SNCC members displayed incredible courage and perseverance, despite being threatened, harassed, beaten, and jailed time and again.

Sit-ins: The first student civil rights campaigns

SNCC came out of the lunch-counter sit-in movement of 1960. Sit-ins were a form of protest in which African American students, sometimes joined by white students, would request service at segregated lunch counters. When they were denied service, they would refuse to leave. The first sit-in of 1960 occurred on February 1, when four African American students at North Carolina A & T (Agricultural and Technological)

Members of SNCC ventured into the most segregated, hostile, and intolerant regions of the deep South to conduct voter registration drives and desegregation campaigns.

College in Greensboro, North Carolina, occupied a Woolworth's Department Store lunch counter. That action captured the imaginations of young people everywhere. Within a week lunch-counter sit-ins were taking place in fifteen cities in five southern states. In the months to come some seventy thousand students would join the sit-in movement.

SNCC founded at Raleigh conference

SNCC was founded by student sit-in activists at a conference held April 16 through 18, 1960, at the predominantly black Shaw University in Raleigh, North Carolina. The conference, convened by veteran civil rights organizer **Ella Baker** (1903–1986; see entry), was attended by over three hundred activists from fifty-six southern colleges and high schools, as well as nineteen northern colleges. Also in attendance were representatives of the Southern Christian Leadership Conference (SCLC), the National Association for the Advancement of Colored People (NAACP), and other established civil rights groups.

Baker recognized the tremendous potential of the student movement to bring about social change and encouraged the students' natural tendency toward democracy—or as she put it, "group-centeredness." Baker was deeply critical of the top-down leadership structure of existing civil rights organizations. Throughout the conference she fended off attempts by the established groups to forge the students into a youth-wing of their respective organizations.

By the end of the conference, SNCC had been defined as an independent organization based on the principles of nonviolence, integration, and racial equality. Its goal was to move the struggle beyond lunch counters, and to achieve racial equality at all levels of society. The majority of SNCC's work was to be carried out by local student groups in their own communities. For the purposes of facilitating communication between branches, a small national office was established in Atlanta, Georgia.

Takes over Freedom Rides

One of the first campaigns in which SNCC became involved as a national organization was the Freedom Rides. The Freedom Rides, initiated by the nonviolent-activist group Congress on Racial Equality (CORE), involved attempts by black and white riders to ride together on interstate (crossing state lines) buses throughout the American South. The purpose of the Freedom Rides was to test the Supreme Court's rulings ordering the desegregation of interstate buses and transportation facilities. On May 4, 1961, thirteen civil rights activists set off on the interstate journey from Washington, D.C., to New Orleans, Louisiana.

The Freedom Riders were met by hostile crowds during the second week of their journey. In Anniston, Alabama, the Freedom Riders' bus was set upon by a mob of whites. The attackers smashed the bus windows with iron bars, tire chains, and clubs, and slashed its tires. A few miles outside of town, they firebombed the bus.

In Birmingham, Alabama, riders were attacked by some thirty white men who had been called to the bus station by the Ku Klux Klan (a group that believes in white supremacy). The men beat the riders viciously with metal pipes and baseball bats. One white rider named James Peck received a serious head injury that required fifty-three stitches to close. Most of the riders were too badly hurt to continue.

SNCC activists, refusing to concede defeat to southern racists, then picked up the torch. SNCC organizers Diane Nash, Lucretia Collins, and Katherine Burke, along with SNCC member and original rider John Lewis (see box), went to Atlanta and Nashville, Tennessee, and recruited an interracial group of twenty-one volunteers to come to Birmingham. On May 20, 1961, the riders began their journey to Jackson, Mississippi. Along the way, in Montgomery, Alabama, riders suffered the worst beatings any had encountered thus far. Jim Zwerg of CORE sustained severe spinal injuries and lost several teeth. John Lewis was knocked unconscious; his bloodied face was pictured in newspapers around the world.

The Freedom Riders arrived in Jackson on May 24 and were promptly arrested for "disturbing the peace." Many riders chose to spend sixty days in jail rather than pay fines.

SNCC enters "closed society" of Mississippi

Following the Freedom Rides, members of SNCC decided to concentrate their energies in Mississippi. That state, nicknamed the "closed society," was undeniably the most seg-

John Lewis: From SNCC to Congress

John Lewis was born on February 21, 1940, in Pike County, Alabama. He was the third of ten children of sharecropper parents. (Sharecropping is a system of farming in which a landless farmer works a plot of land and in return gives the landowner a share of the crop.) Lewis developed an early interest in religion and, as a teenager, was inspired by a radio broadcast of a sermon given by **Martin Luther King, Jr.** (1929–1968; see entry).

After high school Lewis enrolled in the American Baptist Theological Seminary in Nashville, Tennessee. While a student he attended workshops on nonviolence and became active in a newly formed civil rights group, the Nashville Student Movement. In 1960 Lewis and his friends participated in lunch-counter sit-ins.

In April 1960 members of the student sit-in movement from all over the South came together to form the Student Nonviolent Coordinating Committee (SNCC; pronounced "snick"). Lewis joined SNCC shortly after the group's formation. He spent the next six years working with SNCC's desegregation and voting-rights campaigns in numerous rural and urban southern locations and served as SNCC's national chairman from 1963 until 1966.

During the first half of the 1960s Lewis participated in several well-publicized efforts to further the cause of civil rights. In 1961 he embarked on the Freedom Rides— journeys through the South by integrated groups of people, to test the enforcement of a pair of Supreme Court rulings striking down the constitutionality of segregated seating on interstate (crossing state lines) buses and trains. Two years later Lewis worked with members of other civil rights organizations to coordinate the March on Washington for Peace, Jobs, and Justice. And in 1965, while leading hundreds of people over Selma, Alabama's, Edmund Pettus Bridge en route to Montgomery, Lewis had his head cracked open by a police officer's club.

regated state in the Union. Mississippi led the South in the number of killings, beatings, and unexplained disappearances of African American residents.

Mississippi also had the South's lowest percentage of African American voters—just 5 percent were registered in 1960. (In contrast, in Alabama, the state with the next-lowest number of African American voters, 13.7 percent of African Americans were registered.) While African Americans made up

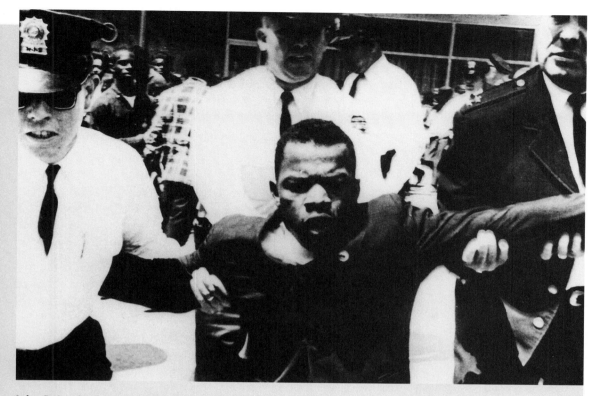

John R. Lewis. *Reproduced by permission of AP/Wide World Photos.*

In 1980 Lewis began his foray into electoral politics. His first victory was to the city council of Atlanta, Georgia. In 1986 he captured the congressional seat from the Georgia district including Atlanta. Today, serving his third term in the U.S. House of Representatives, Lewis continues the fight for social justice.

45 percent of the population in Mississippi, and in some counties outnumbered whites four to one, whites held all the political power. African Americans were kept from registering to vote in Mississippi by literacy tests (tests selectively administered to African American applicants that required would-be voters to read and/or interpret a section of the state Constitution to the satisfaction of the registrar), economic intimidation (such as threats of job loss), and outright violence.

SNCC's civil rights work in Mississippi began in early 1961, when Robert Moses (1935-) and a handful of other SNCC members joined local NAACP activists on a voter registration campaign. Throughout the year civil rights workers were subjected to beatings, arrests, threats, and other forms of intimidation. For all their trouble, they succeeded in adding only a few African Americans to the state's voter rolls.

In 1962 SNCC stepped up its voter registration work in Mississippi. Many SNCC members put their college educations on hold in order to participate full time in the civil rights movement. They moved into small Mississippi towns and forged links with community members. As violence against the activists escalated, SNCC members found they were not only involved in a struggle for civil rights, but in a struggle for their lives.

Freedom Summer

In the fall of 1963 SNCC sponsored the Freedom Vote—a mock election in which African Americans (prevented from voting in real elections) were able to cast ballots for governor and lieutenant governor. SNCC enlisted the help of sixty white students from Yale and Stanford Universities to travel door-to-door and encourage participation in the mock election. SNCC staffers took note that the level of violence against civil rights workers decreased when the white students were present. The Justice Department, SNCC staffers reasoned, had a stake in protecting the lives of upper-middle-class white kids.

Deciding to use that reality to their advantage, SNCC leaders put out the call for volunteers to come to Mississippi in the summer of 1964 to register voters. Approximately a thousand people signed up for the campaign, called Freedom Summer. Most of them were white students from elite northern colleges. Before the volunteers came south, SNCC leaders put them through a week-long training session. They warned the students about the dangers of doing civil rights work in Mississippi and schooled them in techniques of nonviolent action—how to defy authority but not strike back when attacked.

In late June 1964 Freedom Summer volunteers descended upon Mississippi. They conducted door-to-door voter-registration drives and established community centers,

health clinics, legal clinics, and community feeding sites called "freedom kitchens." Volunteers also founded close to fifty "freedom schools" for African American children, at which they taught reading, math, and African American history.

The success of the summer was marred by tragedy. Three Freedom Summer workers—James Chaney, Michael Schwerner, and Andrew Goodman—were killed by Klansmen (members of the Ku Klux Klan, a white supremacist organization) near the town of Philadelphia, Mississippi. The trio disappeared on June 21, and their bodies were found on August 24.

Stokely Carmichael, one of the last leaders of SNCC, addressing a rally at the Mississippi State Capitol.
Reproduced by permission of Corbis Corporation (Bellevue).

Organization divided along philosophical lines

By the fall of 1964 the years of intense activity in the hostile South had taken an emotional toll on SNCC workers. The abuse by white racists had caused some members to question the group's underlying principles of nonviolence and integration. Some SNCC staffers began to carry arms for self-defense, and there was a growing demand to expel the group's white members.

Tensions came to a head at a SNCC leadership meeting in May 1966, at which Stokely Carmichael (1941–1998; later known as Kwame Toure) was elected chairman of the organization. Carmichael promoted separatism (the rejection of white culture and institutions in favor of separate African American culture and institutions) and the carrying of arms. By 1967 SNCC's influence had waned and most of its members had moved on to other groups or other causes.

Sources

Books

Burner, Eric R. *And Gently He Shall Lead Them: Robert Parris Moses and Civil Rights in Mississippi.* New York: New York University Press, 1994.

Burns, Stewart. *Social Movements of the 1960s: Searching for Democracy.* Boston: Twayne Publishers, 1990.

Carson, Clayborne. *In Struggle: SNCC and the Black Awakening of the 1960s.* Cambridge: Harvard University Press, 1981.

Levy, Peter B. *The Civil Rights Movement.* Westwood, CT: Greenwood Press, 1998.

Lewis, John, with Michael D'Orso. *Walking with the Wind: A Memoir of the Movement.* New York: Simon & Schuster, 1998.

Stopper, Emily. *The Student Nonviolent Coordinating Committee: The Growth of Radicalism in a Civil Rights Organization.* Brooklyn, NY: Carlson Publishing, Inc., 1989.

Williams, Juan. *Eyes on the Prize: America's Civil Rights Years, 1954–1965.* New York: Penguin Books, 1987.

Zinn, Howard. *SNCC: The New Abolitionists.* Westport, CT: Greenwood Press, 1985. Originally published by Beacon Press, Boston, 1965.

Students for a Democratic Society

Founded 1960
Ann Arbor, Michigan
Disbanded 1970

**Militant antiwar and antiestablishment
student organization**

Students for a Democratic Society (SDS) was the most promi-nent organization of the New Left: the protest movement of the 1960s in which middle-class college students, most of them from urban or suburban areas, opposed the Vietnam War (1954–75), racial discrimination, and the growing economic gulf between rich and poor. Members of SDS rejected what they considered the materialism and conformity that charac-terized America in the 1950s and promoted "participatory democracy"—a system in which individuals and communities would have a direct voice in shaping the national agenda.

From the drafting of the SDS's philosophical mani-festo, "The Port Huron Statement," in 1962 until 1965, the group concentrated on improving economic conditions in northern ghettos. In the latter half of the 1960s SDS rose to the fore of the burgeoning anti-Vietnam War movement. By the end of the decade SDS had succumbed to factional strife (some of which was fomented by police infiltrators) and extremism. SDS dissolved, and the small core of activists advocating violent revolution formed a new organization called the Weathermen.

Students for a Democratic Society (SDS) was the most powerful and prevalent organization behind the anti-Vietnam War protests that rocked the nation in the latter half of the 1960s.

Students for a Democratic Society (SDS).
Reproduced by permission of Corbis Corporation (Bellevue).

The Port Huron Statement

In June 1962 sixty SDS activists from around the United States gathered at a meeting facility owned by the AFL-CIO (a national labor organization) in Port Huron, Michigan, to define their organization's mission. They produced a sixty-three page political treatise called "The Port Huron Statement." That statement, authored primarily by Tom Hayden, is widely regarded as a classic piece of literature of the New Left.

The Port Huron Statement criticized the American political establishment as being morally bankrupt and oppressive, and took to task the militarism, materialism, and cultural conformity that defined America during the Cold War (the political and military standoff between the United States and Soviet Union from the mid-1940s through the end of the 1980s). The document also spelled out the ideals and principles of SDS—namely the creation of a truly democratic post-Vietnam War society (which they called a "participatory democracy") in which power would be transferred from corporations and government bureaucrats to communities and individuals. It called upon college students throughout the nation to join the movement for social change.

What follows are excerpts from the Port Huron Statement:

> We are people of this generation, bred in at least modest comfort, housed now in universities, looking uncomfortably to the world we inherit.

The founding of SDS

Students for a Democratic Society quietly came into being in 1960. The group had previously existed for several years as the youth wing of the League for Industrial Democracy (LID)—a social democratic labor organization that was influential in the 1930s. SDS's founder, a University of Michigan student named Al Haber, believed that American politicians were essentially war-mongering, racist, and greedy, and that college students held the promise to create change. Haber also felt that the youth organization would have a greater chance to develop if it were independent of the LID. Haber set out to build his organization one student at a time. One of earliest recruits was **Tom Hayden** (1939–; see entry), also a U-M student and editor of the *Michigan Daily*.

When we were kids the United States was the wealthiest and strongest country in the world; . . .

As we grew, however, our comfort was penetrated by events too troubling to dismiss. First, the permeating and victimizing fact of human degradation, symbolized by the Southern struggle against racial bigotry, compelled most of us from silence to activism. Second, the enclosing fact of the Cold War, symbolized by the presence of the Bomb, brought awareness that we ourselves, and our friends, and millions of abstract "others" we knew more directly because of our common peril, might die at any time.

. . . We began to see complicated and disturbing paradoxes in our surrounding America. The declaration "all men are created equal . . . " rang hollow before the facts of Negro life in the South and the big cities of the North. . . .

We regard men as infinitely precious and possessed of unfulfilled capacities for reason, freedom, and love. . . .

Loneliness, estrangement, isolation describe the vast distance between man and man today. These dominant tendencies cannot be overcome by better personnel management, nor by improved gadgets, but only when a love of man overcomes the idolatrous worship of things by man. . . .

We would replace power rooted in possession, privilege, or circumstance by power and uniqueness rooted in love, reflectiveness, reason, and creativity. As a social system we seek the establishment of a democracy of individual participation, governed by two central aims: that the individual share in those social decisions determining the quality and direction of his life; that society be organized to encourage independence in men and provide the media for their common participation.

Haber and Hayden attracted new members to SDS through their involvement in the civil rights movement and by visiting college campuses. By the end of the 1961–62 school year they had signed up a critical core of committed student activists from around the United States. SDS held its first organizational meeting in June 1962. There they defined the group's political aspirations (see box "The Port Huron Statement").

Takes on poverty in northern ghettos

After the Port Huron meeting, SDS decided to put the idea of "participatory democracy" into practice through a program called the Economic Research and Action Project (ERAP). ERAP was intended to address poverty and neglect in ghettos in northern American cities. Some 125 SDS members set up

ERAP operations in nine cities and attempted to organize rent strikes (the refusal to pay rent on a unit until repairs are made) and other measures aimed at forcing negligent landlords and politicians to provide needed services. They also led groups of residents to city halls and police departments to protest police brutality.

The mostly white organizers found it difficult to gain the trust of the mostly African American inner-city dwellers, however, and only in two cities—Newark (New Jersey) and Chicago (Illinois)—did ERAP gain a foothold. By 1967 ERAP's operations were limited to Newark; ERAP closed up shop there in 1967 following that city's explosive race riots.

Shifts emphasis to antiwar activism

In 1965, with the Vietnam War (1954–75) raging, SDS members made the decision to begin antiwar organizing. They objected to U.S. military intervention in the internal affairs of another nation (particularly a small, poor nation halfway around the world), as well as the needless deaths of people on both sides of the conflict.

On April 17, 1965, SDS held its first major antiwar demonstration in Washington, D.C., drawing fifteen thousand people. Seven months later SDS joined forces with other activist groups to bring thirty thousand antiwar protesters to the nation's capital. One result of those demonstrations was that SDS's membership soared; by the end of 1965 the organization had chapters on more than 124 college campuses and over four thousand members.

The antiwar movement gained new momentum in 1966 when President Lyndon Johnson (1908–1973; president 1963–69) declared that college students would no longer be exempted from the draft (prior to that time, draft-age citizens attending college were not made to perform military service). In response to Johnson's decision, SDS held large demonstrations on several campuses. And on April 15, 1967, in New York City, thousands of protesters burned their draft cards at an SDS-sponsored rally. At that time, some thirty thousand students were counted on SDS's membership rolls.

In 1968 members of SDS at Columbia University in New York City helped organize a takeover of five campus

SDS demonstration on election day in 1968 in Washington, D.C.
Reproduced by permission of Corbis Corporation (Bellevue).

buildings by a thousand students. The protest was directed at the university's participation in war-related research, as well as its decision to purchase a city park used by local children for the site on which to build a new gymnasium. Police moved in to clear demonstrators from the buildings, injuring more than 200 students and arresting 712. In the wake of the Columbia action, students at more than forty campuses around the country held building occupations in protest of the war.

Chicago, 1968

In the fall of 1968 many SDS members went to Chicago—the site of the Democratic Party national convention—where thousands of people from around the nation gathered to protest the war, racism, and other issues. Tensions were running particularly high at that time, just months after the assassinations of civil rights leader **Martin Luther King, Jr.,** (1929–1968; see entry) and reformist politician Robert F.

Kennedy (1925–1968). Kennedy, who had been the top Democratic contender for the presidential nomination until his death, had called for an end to the Vietnam War. Hubert Humphrey (1911–1978), the candidate who stood to receive the Democratic Party's nomination at the convention, was less committed to peace.

Nonviolent protests were staged by antiwar activists outside the convention hall. Under orders of Chicago mayor Richard Daley, police indiscriminately beat people, including television and newspaper reporters covering the event. Live television coverage of the convention was interrupted to show the savagery outside the convention hall. The incident was later described in a government report as a "police riot."

Although SDS had not officially endorsed the Chicago protests, the large number of student activists present led many to believe that SDS had organized the event. After the Chicago action SDS membership soared to over one hundred thousand. SDS, however, would not enjoy that popularity for long.

The demise of SDS

The end of SDS began in 1968, when the organization was beset by infighting over tactics and philosophy. Caught up in the revolutionary lingo and fervor of the day, some members believed that a revolution was within reach and that the time was right for violent action. The changes occurring within SDS were illustrated by the declaration of Bernardine Dohrn (elected president of SDS in 1968) that she was a "revolutionary communist." (Communism is a theory of economic and social organization based on the holding of all property in common.)

The tendencies of some SDS members toward extremism were nurtured by the Progressive Labor Party (PLP)—a small, extremist revolutionary political group—whose members began attending SDS meetings. And as formerly "classified" government documents later revealed, much of the tension within SDS was created by police and FBI agents posing as student radicals. By 1969 SDS had become completely dominated by the PLP and other proponents of revolutionary change. One year later SDS was dissolved. A small group of

SDS's most radical former members regrouped into the Weathermen—a revolutionary group that conducted violent actions against selected government and military targets.

"[SDS] caught a mounting wave of youthful revolt in America in the 1960s, rode that wave, and crashed with it," wrote Nancy Zaroulis and Gerald Sullivan in *Who Spoke Up?* (a book chronicling the antiwar movement). " . . . What began with serious political issues of civil rights in the South, poverty in the Northern ghettos, and the war in Vietnam came to embrace every expression of political and countercultural anomie. . . . Vaguely defined notions of participatory democracy and open, endless debate, combined with a disdain for old-fashioned parliamentary procedure, produced within SDS a ruling elite created in the image of its own exotic rhetoric. Style without substance became the SDS hallmark. . . . The rhetoric became increasingly shrill. . . . This, in turn, led rapidly to the alienation of the common folk of SDS."

Sources

Books

Anderson, Terry H. *The Movement and the Sixties: Protest in America from Greensboro to Wounded Knee*. New York: Oxford University Press, 1995.

Burns, Stewart. *Social Movements of the 1960s*. Boston: Twayne Publishers, 1990.

Gitlin, Todd. *The Sixties: Years of Hope, Days of Rage*. New York: Bantam Books, 1987.

Hamilton, Neil A. *The ABC-CLIO Companion to The 1960s Counterculture in America*. Santa Barbara, CA: ABC-CLIO, 1997, pp. 245–47, 292–93.

Layman, Richard, ed. *American Decades: 1960–1969*. Detroit: Gale Research, Inc., 1995, pp. 239–41.

McGuire, Willliam, and Leslie Wheeler. *American Social Leaders*. Santa Barbara, CA: ABC-CLIO, 1993, pp. 223–24.

Miller, James. *Democracy Is in the Streets: From Port Huron to the Siege of Chicago*. New York: Simon & Schuster, Inc., 1987.

Zaroulis, Nancy, and Gerald Sullivan. *Who Spoke Up? American Protest against the War in Vietnam, 1963–1975*. Garden City, NY: Doubleday, 1984.

Articles

Hunt, Charles W. Review of "'Democracy Is in the Streets': From Port Huron to the Siege of Chicago." *Monthly Review.* September 1989: 58+.

Web Sites

Port Huron Statement. [Online] Available http://lists.village.virginia.edu/sixties/HTML_docs/Resources/Primary/Manifestos/SDS_Port_Huron.html (accessed April 15, 2000).

Aung San Suu Kyi

Born June 19, 1945
Yangon (formerly Rangoon),
Myanmar (formerly Burma)

Prodemocracy activist

Although Aung San Suu Kyi spent most of her life outside of her native Burma, she always believed that she would some day be called back to serve her people. Being the daughter of the famous general Aung San, who was widely regarded as the father of Burma, Suu Kyi believed she was born with a responsibility to honor her father's legacy.

Suu Kyi's activism on behalf of the Burmese people began in 1988, when she returned to Burma to care for her sick mother. Unable to ignore the massive street demonstrations against government repression and corruption, and the brutal killings of protesters by soldiers, Suu Kyi lent her voice to the resistance. She immediately became the accepted leader of the Burmese opposition movement. Because of her courageous stand against the military government, Suu Kyi was placed under house arrest for six years. During that time she received the Nobel Peace Prize. Suu Kyi remains an international symbol of hope for a democratic Burma (which in 1989 was renamed Myanmar).

Daughter of the "father of modern Burma"

Aung San Suu Kyi [pronounced Aung Sahn Sue Chee] was born on June 19, 1945, in Rangoon (since renamed Yan-

"She became the leader of a democratic opposition which employs nonviolent means to resist a regime characterized by brutality. Suu Kyi's struggle is one of the most extraordinary examples of civil courage in Asia in recent decades."

Nobel Committee, upon granting the Peace Prize to Aung San Suu Kyi on October 14, 1991.

Aung San Suu Kyi.
Courtesy of the Library of Congress.

gon), the capital city of Burma. She was the youngest of three children, and the only girl, born to Aung San and Khin Kyi. Her name—a combination of those of her mother, father, and paternal grandfather—means "A Bright Collection of Strange Victories."

Suu Kyi's father, General Aung San, was the leader of the movement for Burmese independence from British colonial rule. He was head of the transitional Burmese government while negotiating the terms of the nation's independence. Suu Kyi never knew her father, because he (along was eight colleagues) was assassinated by a political rival in July 1947, just six months before the official end of colonial rule. Aung San remains the most celebrated hero in Burmese history.

The greatest tragedy in young Suu Kyi's life, however, occurred when she was seven years old. That year she witnessed the drowning death of her older brother, to whom she was particularly close.

Accompanies mother on diplomatic mission to India

In 1960 Suu Kyi moved to India with her mother, who had been named the Burmese ambassador to that nation (she had previously been chair of Burma's Council of Social Services). Khin Kyi's appointment marked the first time a woman had been selected to head a Burmese diplomatic mission. Suu Kyi and her mother resided in a beautiful home in New Delhi and lived a life of luxury. Suu Kyi attended an exclusive school and learned to play the piano and ride horses. Perhaps the greatest lessons Suu Kyi learned during her years in India were the teachings of **Mohandas Gandhi** (1869–1948; see entry). Gandhi, the leader of the Indian independence movement, had been a proponent of changing unjust systems through peaceful means.

While Suu Kyi and her mother were in India, a general named Ne Win took power in Burma in a military coup. During his twenty-six year dictatorship, from 1962 to 1988, Ne Win ruled Burma by violence and intimidation. Political dissent of any form was not tolerated. His economic policies were disastrous, as evidenced by the decline in average yearly Burmese earnings from $670 in 1960 to $200 in 1988.

Oxford University, marriage, and motherhood

Suu Kyi began her college career in India, attending for short periods Lady Sri Ram College and Delhi University. In 1964 she moved to England to study politics, philosophy, and economics at St. Hugh's College of Oxford University. There she met Michael Aris, a British scholar of Tibetan civilization, whom she would later marry. After receiving her bachelor of arts degree in 1967, Suu Kyi worked as a teacher at an English preparatory school and as a research assistant for a Burma scholar at London University. In 1969 she began working in New York City at the United Nations Advisory Committee on Administrative and Budgetary Questions.

On New Year's Day, 1972, Suu Kyi wed Aris in a Buddhist ceremony. The couple then moved to Bhutan, a small kingdom in the Himalayas, northwest of Burma, where Aris had been working as a tutor for the royal family. Suu Kyi found employment with the Bhutanese Foreign Ministry.

A year later Suu Kyi and Aris returned to London, where Suu Kyi gave birth to their first son, Alexander. After Aris completed his dissertation, the family moved to Oxford so Aris could teach at Oxford University. Suu Kyi stayed home and cared for Alexander and in 1977 gave birth to her second son, Kim. Even while mothering her young children, Suu Kyi read extensively and learned Japanese.

Researches father's life in Japan

Over the years, Suu Kyi's interest in her father deepened. She first conducted research on his life for a biography titled *Aung San,* published in 1984. The following year, intent on learning more about Aung San, she traveled to the University of Kyoto in Japan as a visiting scholar. There, with Kim in tow, she interviewed people who had known her father and studied papers recounting Aung San's trips to Japan.

In 1986 Suu Kyi and Kim joined Michael and Alexander in Simla, in northern India, where Michael was a visiting fellow at the Indian Institute of Advanced Study. Suu Kyi also found a position at the institute, which in 1990 published her book titled *Burma and India: Some Aspects of Intellectual Life under Colonialism.* In 1987 the family returned to England. Suu Kyi applied and was accepted to a doctoral program in

Burmese literature at the School of Oriental and Asian Studies at London University.

Returns to Burma to care for mother

Suu Kyi put her academic plans on hold on March 31, 1988, when she learned that her mother had had a serious stroke. Suu Kyi immediately packed her bags and headed for Burma. Little did she know that her life would be changed forever.

Suu Kyi returned to her homeland to find that political tensions were running high. An incident between college students and riot police had caused long-simmering discontent over the military government's policies to erupt in violence. More than a thousand students were killed and thousands of others were wounded or jailed in the ensuing protests. Matters were made worse that August, when a government devaluation of the currency wiped out the savings of rich and poor alike.

Gets involved in opposition movement

The largest demonstration of the summer began on August 8, 1988, at eight minutes past eight o'clock in the morning (for that reason it is called the 8–8–88 protest). More than a million people throughout the nation participated in work stoppages, marches, and rallies. They carried large, framed pictures of General Aung San, Suu Kyi's father. Over the next three days the armed forces shot into crowds of unarmed people, killing more than three thousand.

Suu Kyi had not participated in the 8–8–88 protest, but after the killings she could no longer remain on the sidelines of the conflict. "This great struggle has arisen from the intense and deep desire of the people for a fully democratic parliamentary system," stated Suu Kyi in a 1997 interview with *The Humanist*. "I could not, as my father's daughter, remain indifferent to all that was going on."

Suu Kyi made her first public address on August 26, at Shwedagon Pagoda, Burma's most sacred shrine. Word that Aung San's daughter would speak brought out a crowd of between five hundred thousand and one million people. Suu Kyi spoke about her father's belief in democracy and the importance of the current uprising. "This national crisis could in fact be called the second struggle for national independence," she stated. Suu Kyi advocated nonviolence, free and fair elections, and a "revolution of the spirit" of the Burmese people.

Suu Kyi brought focus to the opposition movement, which to that point had been united only by a desire to bring down the military government. She was immediately acknowledged as the leader of prodemocracy forces.

Military government tightens grip on country

The next month the military government regrouped under the name State Law and Order Restoration Council (SLORC) and banned all demonstrations and political gatherings of more than four people. The rulers also claimed the right to arrest and sentence dissidents without trial. The armed forces were ordered to show no mercy for people who violated the rules; thousands of people were massacred in the streets and thousands more were jailed and tortured.

On a seemingly contradictory note, the SLORC permitted the formation of political parties and promised to hold free elections in 1990. Suu Kyi took advantage of the opportunity and formed a party called the National League for Democracy (NLD). As secretary-general of the NLD, Suu Kyi toured the nation and spoke out for human rights and democracy (an activity that violated the government ban on political gatherings). Throughout her travels Suu Kyi faced government harassment. Her supporters were arrested, she was accused of being a communist, and false allegations were made about her personal life. The government's strategy backfired—Suu Kyi's popularity grew and within a year the NLD boasted two million members (in a nation of forty million people).

Suu Kyi came close to death on April 5, 1989, while campaigning for the NLD. Six soldiers who had been given orders to kill Suu Kyi jumped from a jeep, kneeled, and prepared to fire. Suu Kyi emerged from the crowd that had gathered around her and shooed away her supporters. She then walked directly toward the soldiers, presenting them with a clear shot. At the last moment, the commanding officer rescinded the order to shoot.

When Suu Kyi was placed under house arrest by the Burmese government, supporters rallied outside her home.
Reproduced by permission of Corbis Corporation (Bellevue).

Suu Kyi downplayed her courageous stand. "It seemed so much simpler to provide them with a single target," she later stated, "than to bring everyone else in."

Placed under house arrest

On July 20, 1989, Suu Kyi was placed under house arrest. To prevent her from leaving or visitors from coming, her home was surrounded by tanks and barbed wire. Soldiers with bayonets were stationed outside her door. On the same day of Suu Kyi's detainment, forty-two other NLD leaders were arrested and NLD offices were ransacked. Suu Kyi protested the crackdown by staging a hunger strike from July 20 through mid-August.

In January 1990 the government forbade any further visits from Suu Kyi's family members and cut her off from all written communication. They also removed her name from the ballot in the upcoming election (that move overturned the electoral commission's previous approval of Suu Kyi's candidacy for president on the NLD slate). Several times officials offered to free Suu Kyi, in exchange for her promise to leave the country and never return. Suu Kyi steadfastly refused those offers. Confined to her house, she passed the time reading, praying, and sewing.

Government nullifies election

The NLD won a landslide in the elections of May 1990, taking 392 out of 485 seats for parliament. Rather than transferring power as promised, military leaders nullified the election and imprisoned many of the victorious NLD candidates. They instituted a crackdown on political activities nationwide. Had the government not thwarted the democratic process, Suu Kyi would have likely been made president of the country with her NLD in control of the parliament.

Wins awards for peace

Even while treated as an outlaw in her own country, Suu Kyi's esteem rose in the international community. She won several awards in the early 1990s for her work promoting democracy, including the Thorolf Rafto Memorial Prize for Human Rights, the European Parliament's Sakharov Prize for Freedom of Thought, and the Marisa Bellisario Prize.

In 1991 Suu Kyi was awarded the most prestigious honor: the Nobel Peace Prize. Burmese military officials cynically offered her the chance to travel to Norway to accept her prize, but only if she promised not to return. Despite an overwhelming desire to see her husband and sons, and to accept the prestigious award, Suu Kyi declined.

Suu Kyi's sons accepted the award on their mother's behalf. Alexander, then sixteen years old, said that his mother "would say this prize belongs not to her but to all those men, women and children who, even as I speak, continue to sacrifice their well being, their freedom and their lives in pursuit of a democratic Burma. Speaking as her son, I would add that I personally believe that by her own dedication and personal sacrifice she has come to be a worthy symbol through whom the plight of all the people of Burma may be recognized."

"Freedom from Fear"

The year 1991 saw the publication of *Freedom from Fear and Other Writings*—a collection of essays by and about Suu Kyi, compiled and edited by her husband, Michael Aris. "The quintessential revolution is that of the spirit, born of an intellectual conviction of the need for change in those mental attitudes and values which shape the course of a nation's development," wrote Suu Kyi in the title essay, "Freedom from Fear." "A revolution which aims merely at changing official policies and institutions with a view to an improvement in material conditions has little chance of genuine success.

"It is not enough merely to call for freedom, democracy, and human rights. There has to be a united determination to persevere in the struggle, to make sacrifices in the name of enduring truths, to resist the corrupting influences of desire, ill will, ignorance, and fear. Among the basic freedoms to which men aspire that their lives might be full and uncramped, freedom from fear stands out as both a means and an end."

Government lifts house arrest, continues restrictions

On July 11, 1995, Suu Kyi's six-year-long sentence to house arrest was lifted. She immediately resumed her role as opposition leader, addressing large crowds of supporters. After Suu Kyi's release, however, the military leaders again clamped down on the activities of NLD members. Many dissidents were jailed and tortured. Suu Kyi's phone line was tapped and her ability to travel within the country was restricted. "Nothing has changed since my release," Suu Kyi told *The Humanist* four months after her release. "Let the world know that we are still prisoners in our own country."

Despite government attempts to silence her, Suu Kyi managed to deliver the keynote address to the September 1995 United Nations World Conference on Women, in Beijing, China, via a videotape smuggled out of Burma. And in June 1996 Suu Kyi hosted a three-day meeting of the NLD that was attended by ten thousand party members. Two hundred and sixty-two attendees were arrested and later released.

Repression against Suu Kyi escalates

In November 1996 the repression against Suu Kyi escalated into a physical attack. She was on her way to visit supporters when military-affiliated thugs stoned her car and smashed her windshield with an iron bar. Soldiers stationed nearby did not intervene to stop the attack.

In early 1997 government restrictions against Suu Kyi placed her in an unofficial state of house arrest. Suu Kyi was no longer allowed to make speeches and soldiers erected barricades in the street outside her house. When assistants and bodyguards came or went from her house, they were subject to arrest.

Suu Kyi refused to be silenced by those repressive measures. In September 1997 she held an NLD meeting that was attended by some eight hundred party members. Dozens of other would-be attendees were arrested en route to the meeting.

Government denies Suu Kyi final visit with husband

Suu Kyi suffered a personal tragedy on March 27, 1999, when her husband died of cancer. To make matters worse, she had not been allowed to see her husband before his death. When Michael Aris had learned about his fatal illness he had applied for a visa to Burma. It would have been his first visit in three years. The government denied his request, suggesting that Suu Kyi visit her husband in England instead. Suu Kyi, however, knew that if she left Burma she would most likely never be allowed back.

"There can be few greater sacrifices for one's country than to forsake husband and children for an unequal struggle against tyranny," stated *The Economist* on April 3, 1999. "Miss Suu Kyi's stubbornness is one of the few beacons in Myanmar's gloom."

Sources

Books

Aung San Suu Kyi. *Freedom from Fear and Other Writings*. Edited by Michael Aris. New York: Viking, 1991.

"Aung San Suu Kyi." *Current Biography Yearbook*. Edited by Judith Graham. New York: H. W. Wilson Company, 1992, pp. 27–31.

Parenteau, John. *Prisoner for Peace: Aung San Suu Kyi and Burma's Struggle for Democracy.* Greensboro, NC: Morgan Reynolds, Inc., 1994.

Articles

Benjamin, Daniel. "A Country under the Boot: One Year after Explosive Riots, the Regime Cracks Down on Pro-Democracy Activists." *Time.* August 21, 1989: 36+.

Clements, Alan. "We Are Still Prisoners in Our Own Country: An Interview with Aung San Suu Kyi." *The Humanist.* November-December, 1997: 15+.

"A Glimmer of Hope? Myanmar." *The Economist.* October 4, 1997: 45+.

Kean, Leslie, and Dennis Bernstein. "Aung San Suu Kyi." (Interview.) *The Progressive.* March 1997: 32+.

Nelan, Bruce W. "Heroine in Chains." *Time.* October 28, 1991: 73.

"Shame in Myanmar." *The Economist.* April 3, 1999: 13.

Spaeth, Anthony. "Setting Free 'The Lady': Aung San Suu Kyi Is Released after Six Years of House Arrest. But How Far Will Her Freedom Go?" *Time.* July 24, 1995: 48.

John Trudell

Born 1947
Niobrara, Nebraska

Native American activist, musician, and actor

John Trudell has been one of the leading voices for Native American rights for thirty years. Trudell's entry into the struggle for equality began in 1969, with the takeover of Alcatraz Island (an island in San Francisco [California] Bay). Soon thereafter Trudell joined the American Indian Movement (**AIM**; see entry); he served as the group's cochairman and national spokesperson from 1973 to 1979. In 1979 Trudell suffered a tremendous personal tragedy when his wife, children, and mother-in-law burned to death in an arson fire. Many people believe that the killings were instigated by law enforcement officials as punishment for Trudell's political activities

The road to activism

Details about Trudell's early years are sketchy. What is known is that he was born and raised on the Santee Sioux Reservation in Niobrara, Nebraska (in northeastern Nebraska on the border of South Dakota). Trudell never learned the identity of his mother. His father was a Santee Sioux named Thurman Clifford Trudell.

"If people in this country really want to know how to help the Indian people, they must learn to help themselves."

John Trudell in 1992 interview with Billboard *magazine.*

John Trudell.
Reproduced by permission of AP/Wide World Photos.

Trudell served in the navy for four years during the Vietnam War (1954–75). He was deeply disturbed by the racism he witnessed in the armed forces, both directed at minority U.S. servicemen and at the Vietnamese people. When Trudell finished his tour of duty he moved to California. There he married a woman named Lou and had two daughters, Maurie and Tara. He also became involved in the budding Indian rights movement.

Occupies Alcatraz Island

In November 1969 Trudell and his family joined the activist group Indians of All Tribes (IAT) in their takeover of Alcatraz Island, the former penal colony in the San Francisco Bay. The occupiers demanded that the island, which had once been populated by Native Americans, be given back to Native Americans. They cited the 1868 Treaty of Fort Laramie with the Sioux Indians, which stipulated that abandoned federal properties on former Native American lands were to be returned to Native Americans. The IAT made plans to convert the island into a spiritual, cultural, and educational center for Native Americans.

The Trudell family remained on Alcatraz for the nineteen months of the occupation. During that time Trudell coordinated publicity efforts for the IAT. He spoke at press conferences and hosted a daily radio program called *Radio Free Alcatraz*, broadcast on KPFA-FM in Berkeley, California. John and Lou's daughter, Wovoka, was born on the island. (Wovoka was named after a nineteenth-century Paiute spiritual leader.)

In June 1971 the Native Americans were forced off the island during a raid by federal agents. The U.S. government subsequently annexed Alcatraz to the Golden Gate National Recreation Area. The occupation of Alcatraz thrust the Indian rights movement into the national spotlight. It inspired a generation of Native Americans to stand up for their rights and touched off a decade-long struggle for the recognition of treaty rights, self-determination, and the return of Native American lands.

Joins AIM at Mount Rushmore and Plymouth Rock

While on Alcatraz, Trudell became involved with the American Indian Movement (AIM)—a militant Indian rights group, founded in 1968, that fought for the return of tribal lands, enforcement of government treaties, respect for Native American human rights, and greater economic opportunities for Native Americans. Throughout the 1970s Trudell's life revolved around AIM activities.

In September 1970 Trudell took leave from Alcatraz to help coordinate a demonstration at Mount Rushmore in the Black Hills of South Dakota. Together with AIM activist Russell Means and a University of California-Berkeley doctoral student named Lee Brightman, Trudell led about fifty Native Americans to the top of Mount Rushmore. The group demanded that all lands in South Dakota west of the Missouri River, including Mount Rushmore and the rest of the Black Hills, be returned to the Sioux in accordance with the Treaty of Fort Laramie. The demonstration received national news coverage. While Trudell returned to Alcatraz, others in the group remained camped out on the mountaintop until brutal winter storms struck (see AIM entry).

In November 1970 Trudell led a group of activists from Alcatraz to a living history museum called Plimoth Plantation (near Martha's Vineyard and the original Plymouth Colony in Massachusetts) for an AIM-sponsored Thanksgiving Day protest. AIM had come to Plimoth at the invitation of Wampanoag Indians, whose ancestors, they claimed, had been massacred by the Pilgrims after helping the settlers survive for their first two years on the North American continent. The descendants of the surviving Wampanoags wanted to publicize their understanding of Thanksgiving—that the holiday had begun as a celebration of the massacre of Native Americans.

The Native American protesters held a march along the highway to Plimoth Plantation, disrupted the feast underway in the village hall, then took over a replica of the *Mayflower* (the ship on which the original pilgrims came to America) docked at the harbor. Late that night Trudell and a few others scaled the protective fence around the Plymouth Rock monument and bathed the rock in red paint, which symbolized the spilled blood of the Wampanoag Indians.

Participates in the Trail of Broken Treaties

In the fall of 1972 Trudell participated in AIM's occupation of the Bureau of Indian Affairs (BIA) headquarters in

Washington, D.C. The demonstration, called the Trail of Broken Treaties, started out on the American West Coast. A caravan of cars, trucks, and buses picked up Native Americans at reservations along the way to Washington, D.C. AIM had written to the BIA ahead of time, informing the organization of the coming convergence on Washington and presenting its list of twenty demands. Among AIM's demands were restoration of the tribes' treaty-making status, the return of stolen Native American lands, and the revocation of state government authority over Indian affairs. AIM also asked for the opportunity to address a joint session of Congress.

When the delegation arrived at the BIA, it was turned away at the door. In response, the Native Americans took over the building and kicked out BIA employees. The occupation lasted six days. During that time protesters destroyed BIA property and smuggled out files containing evidence of BIA corruption.

The siege came to an end when protesters accepted the government's offer of immunity from prosecution, funds for their transportation home, and consideration of AIM's demands. The government later rejected every point on AIM's list.

Comes under FBI scrutiny

Throughout the occupation of BIA headquarters, Trudell served as a spokesperson for AIM. As a result of his high-profile position, Trudell came under increased scrutiny by the Federal Bureau of Investigation's (FBI) Counterintelligence Program. (COINTELPRO—the secret FBI operation in the 1960s and 1970s in which FBI agents, under the guise of combating domestic terrorism, gathered information on and attempted to destroy the anti-Vietnam War movement, the civil rights movement, and militant organizations of people of color.) In 1986, when Trudell obtained his FBI file under the Freedom of Information Act, he discovered that the FBI had labeled him an "extremely effective agitator." Trudell eventually received seventeen thousand pages of information the FBI had collected on him between the years 1969 and 1979.

In 1973 Trudell was elected to the cochairmanship of AIM, a position that he held until 1979. His marriage to Lou Trudell having ended a couple of years earlier, Trudell wed again, this time an activist from the Duck Valley Reservation in Nevada named Tina Manning.

Aids Leonard Peltier

In 1975 Trudell turned his energies to defending fellow-AIM activist Leonard Peltier (1944–), who had been charged with, and later convicted of, the murders of two FBI agents on the Pine Ridge Reservation. Peltier had been on the reservation offering protection to Lakota traditionalists (adherents of traditional Native American religion and culture) from attacks by the tribal police when a firefight erupted between FBI agents and Indians.

Peltier was convicted by an all-white jury in a highly controversial trial punctuated by coerced statements from prosecution witnesses, fabricated evidence, and "judge-shopping" (the prosecution manipulated the court system to secure a judge with a known anti-Indian bias). Trudell is among the many people who believe Peltier was framed for the killings

"FBI agents armed with M-16s came onto the Pine Ridge Reservation to serve a warrant they didn't have," Trudell stated to the press regarding the FBI manhunt in the wake of the shoot-out, "on someone who wasn't there; they were accompanied by over fifty highly trained military marksmen, also with high-powered automatic weapons. These agents opened fire on a small house in which men, women, and children were asleep."

Peltier is presently serving two life sentences in Leavenworth Federal Prison in Kansas. Trudell continues to speak out against the illegality of the FBI presence on the reservation, as well the gross miscarriage of justice in Peltier's trial.

Family dies in arson fire

In February 1979, when Trudell was in Washington protesting the Peltier case and other abuses against Native Americans, tragedy struck. An arson fire at Trudell's home (the perpetrator of which was never caught) claimed the lives of his wife Tina, the couple's three children—Ricarda Star, Sunshine Karma, and Eli Changing Sun—and Tina's mother Leah Manning.

Charlene Teters Takes on Indian Mascot Issue

Representative of today's AIM activists is Native American artist, educator, and writer Charlene Teters (1952–). Teters, who is also a spokesperson for the National Coalition on Racism in Sports and Media (NCRSM), concentrates her energies on the struggle to stop the use of Native American imagery as sports-team mascots. Teters became involved in the Native American mascot issue in the late 1980s while a graduate student at the University of Illinois (U of I). There Teters learned the dehumanizing effects of U of I's fictitious Indian chief mascot, Chief Illiniwek.

Teters compares Native American caricatures to stereotypical symbols of other racial groups. "These images should have gone by the wayside along with Little Black Sambo and the Frito Bandito," stated Teters in the video documentary *In Whose Honor?* "If it was any other religious practice that was being abused, we would hear about it. We would certainly hear about it if it was some kind of distortion of a Catholic ceremony or Jewish ceremony . . . . But somehow because it is a Native practice and ceremony and religious items, it is not respected."

In 1991, while living in Washington, D.C., Teters organized protests at Washington Redskins football games. (The term "redskin" is widely considered one of the most blatantly racist terms for Native Americans.) The coalition of organizations

Just twelve hours before the arson attack, Trudell had burned an upside-down American flag on the steps of the FBI building and had been arrested. Many people believe that the killing of Trudell's family was orchestrated by the FBI in retribution for the flag-burning, as well as for Trudell's years of activism and exposure of FBI abuses on the Pine Ridge Reservation.

After the killing of his family, Trudell began writing poetry. He published a book of poems in 1981, titled *Living in Reality*. In the coming years Trudell would turn some of those poems into songs.

Launches career in music and film

Since the 1980s Trudell has made a name for himself in the music and movie industries. Trudell's film debut was a

Charlene Teters. *Reproduced by permission.*

that participated in the protests—including the National Congress of American Indians, the National Organization for Women, and the National Association for the Advancement of Colored People, among others—came together to form the NCRSM. NCRSM continues to draw attention to the racist imagery of the Atlanta Braves, the Kansas City Chiefs, the Cleveland Indians, and other teams with Indian mascots or nicknames.

"Our people paid with their lives to keep what little we have left," stated Teters in *In Whose Honor?* "The fact that we even have anything today speaks to the strength of our ancestors, and that is what I'm protecting."

cameo appearance in the 1989 Hand Made Films production *Powwow Highway.* He took on larger roles in two 1992 films, *Incident at Oglala: The Leonard Peltier Story* and *Thunderheart,* both by British director Michael Apted, about events on the Pine Ridge Reservation.

"[Trudell] was an inspiration to me in making the documentary film *Incident at Oglala,*" stated Apted in a promotional release, "about Leonard Peltier's fight for justice. . . . There wasn't an untruthful moment in his performance. 'Sometimes they have to kill us,' he told me, 'because they cannot break our spirit.' John is one of those rare unbreakable spirits."

Trudell launched his musical career in 1979. Known in the music industry as a rock-poet, Trudell calls his musical style "modern electric song." His songs combine his political convictions and spiritual beliefs and are set to the tempo of traditional Indian chants. His spoken lyrics are accompanied by traditional vocals and instrumentation.

Trudell released his first commercial recording, titled *aka Graffiti Man,* on the independent label Rykodisc in 1992. (He began recording music for his own Peace Label in 1982.) His second major release, *Johnny Damas and Me,* came in 1994 and is also with Rykodisc. Both recordings have been met with widespread critical acclaim. Trudell continues to promote Native American rights during his on-stage performances.

"If people in this country really want to know how to help the Indian people," stated Trudell in a 1992 interview with *Billboard* magazine, "they must learn to help themselves. Because the wheel has turned to where all the things we've suffered are now becoming the norm of the average citizen: the lack of representation, the political deception, the ethnic and class discrimination, the loss of jobs and health and property."

Sources

Books

Churchill, Ward, and Jim Vander Wall. *Agents of Repression: The FBI's Secret Wars against the Black Panther Party and the American Indian Movement.* Boston: South End Press, 1988.

Malinowski, Sharon, and Simon Glickman, eds. *Native North American Biography.* Detroit: U•X•L, 1996, pages 377–79.

Matthiessen, Peter. *In the Spirit of Crazy Horse.* New York: Viking Press, 1980.

Means, Russell, and Marvin J. Wolf. *Where White Men Fear to Tread: The Autobiography of Russell Means.* New York: St. Martin's Press, 1995.

Smith, Paul Chaat, and Robert Allen Warrior. *Like a Hurricane: The Indian Movement from Alcatraz to Wounded Knee.* New York: The New Press, 1995.

Articles

Johnson, Brian D. Review of "Thunderheart." *Maclean's.* April 13, 1992: 71.

Sprague, David. "Trudell Inspires Unusual Ryko Promo." *Billboard.* January 29, 1994: 13+.

White, Timothy. "Native American Song, Then & Now." *Billboard.* May 9, 1992: 5.

Videos

Apted, Michael, director. *Incident at Oglala: The Leonard Peltier Story* (documentary). Miramax, 1992.

Apted, Michael, director. *Thunderheart*. Columbia, 1992.

Rosenstein, Jay, writer and director. *In Whose Honor?* Champaign, IL: Smoking Munchkin Video, 1997.

Web Sites

John Trudell home page. [Online] Available http://www.planet-peace.org/trudell/index1.html (accessed December 1, 1999).

Townsend, Lori. Interview with John Trudell by Lori Townsend of WOJB (Kyle, South Dakota). February 28, 1998. [Online] Available http://www.dickshovel.com/lsa13.html (accessed January 14, 1999).

Harriet Tubman

Born 1820 or 1821
Dorchester County, Maryland
Died March 10, 1913
Auburn, New York

Fugitive slave, abolitionist, Underground Railroad conductor, and Union army spy

"When I found I had crossed that line [to freedom], I looked at my hands to see if I was the same person. There was such a glory over everything."

Harriet Tubman to her biographer, Sarah H. Bradford

Harriet Tubman.
Reproduced by permission of Corbis Corporation (Bellevue).

Harriet Tubman, an escaped slave, was the most famous of all "conductors" on the Underground Railroad. The Underground Railroad was an elaborate system of safe houses and secret routes through which slaves escaped to freedom beginning in the 1840s. The escape routes stretched from southern slave states (primarily Kentucky, Delaware, and Maryland), to northern states and Canada, where slavery was illegal. "Conductors" were people who ventured into the American South to pick up slaves and lead them to freedom.

After her escape in 1849, Tubman returned to the South nineteen times and rescued hundreds of slaves. Among the slaves she liberated were her elderly parents and ten of her brothers and sisters. Tubman never lost a passenger. She was never captured, despite a $40 thousand bounty placed on her head by slave owners. Tubman was considered the "Moses" of her people because, like the biblical Moses, she led her people to freedom.

Early years as a slave

Harriet Tubman was one of eleven children born to plantation slaves Benjamin Ross and Harriet Green. Like her parents and siblings, Tubman was the "property" of plantation owner Edward Brodas. Brodas originally named the newborn child Araminta Ross; her mother called her Minty.

As a young child, Tubman was looked after by elderly slave women while her mother worked in the field. At the age of six Tubman was sent off the plantation to work for a white couple, the Cooks. One of Tubman's jobs was to check muskrat traps in the river. After one year the Cooks returned Tubman, who had contracted measles, to the Brodas plantation.

After regaining her health, Tubman was hired out again—this time to a white woman named Miss Susan. Tubman's job was to clean Miss Susan's house and take care of her baby. If the child's crying woke up Miss Susan in the night, or if Tubman somehow failed in her daytime duties, Miss Susan lashed her with a cowhide whip. One day, caught in the act of stealing from the sugar bowl, Tubman ran away and hid in a pigsty to escape a whipping. Shortly thereafter Tubman, suffering from a lack of food and sleep and scarred from the whippings, was returned to the Brodas plantation.

Works hard in the fields

Deemed untrainable as a house slave, young Tubman was sent to the fields to work. Despite her small stature, Tubman was ordered to chop wood and haul heavy loads. When she could not perform her tasks, she was whipped. At age eleven Tubman began wearing a brightly colored scarf on her head, signifying (according to slave custom) that she was no longer a child. At that time she took on her mother's name: Harriet. Years of hard work in the fields had made Tubman very strong, and capable of working long hours and lifting heavy loads.

As a young teenager, Tubman was hired out by her master to harvest crops on a neighbor's farm. One evening, as the slaves were working in the fields, Tubman saw a slave sneaking away. She also noticed the plantation's overseer in pursuit of the slave. Tubman tried to alert the slave; in response, the overseer struck Tubman in the head with a two-pound iron weight. The wound scarred Tubman's forehead. Due to the injury, for the rest of her life she would suffer from seizures that would cause her to fall asleep for brief periods of time.

After recovering, Tubman went back to work on the Brodas plantation. In 1836 Brodas allowed Tubman to "hire her time"—an arrangement by which Tubman paid Brodas $75 a year and was allowed to keep the wages she made working for other people.

In 1844 Tubman married John Tubman, a free black man (one of the sixty-two thousand free blacks in the state of Maryland at the time; there were ninety-two thousand slaves). Tubman moved into John's cabin but was not happy. She longed for freedom and dreamed of escaping to the North.

Escapes to the North

Tubman's master died in 1849. Fearing that she would be sold to the deep South to pick cotton, Tubman decided to escape to the North. After two days of running and hiding Tubman sought help from a local Quaker woman who was known for aiding fugitive slaves. (The Quakers, or Society of Friends, is a religious organization that stresses nonviolence and simple living.) The woman told Tubman about two families along the road to the north that would give her food and shelter. Tubman had heard talk of an "underground railroad" that slaves could take to freedom in the North. She was finally a passenger on the railroad.

Tubman traveled by night, using the North Star as her guide, and hid during the day. After traveling through ninety miles of swamp and woodland she finally reached the Mason-Dixon line, the boundary between Maryland and Pennsylvania (and between the slave South and the free North). Tubman headed to Philadelphia, Pennsylvania, home to a large population of free blacks, where she found work washing dishes in a hotel kitchen.

Becomes Underground Railroad conductor

In 1850, with the passage of the Fugitive Slave Act, Tubman was no longer safe in the "free" North. Under this federal law, any African American person could be accused of being a runaway slave and brought before a federal judge. Accused runaways were denied a jury trial and could not testify on their own behalf. The law also made it a federal crime to aid or harbor a fugitive slave and provided strict penalties

for helping a slave escape. Those who benefitted most from the law were professional slave catchers, who for a fee captured runaway slaves and returned them to their owners. Always a grave threat to fugitive slaves and free blacks in the South, slave catchers beginning in 1850 operated boldly in the North.

After the passage of the Fugitive Slave Act many fugitive slaves and free blacks fled to Canada, where slavery had been abolished in 1833. Tubman, in contrast, headed south, back into slave territory. She was determined to help other slaves escape to freedom. Over the next ten years Tubman made at least nineteen trips into the South and escorted over three hundred slaves to Canada and freedom. In between rescue missions to the South, Tubman worked at odd jobs to earn money for her next trip.

In 1851 Tubman tried to bring her husband, John Tubman, to the North. She boldly traveled to Dorchester County, Maryland, only to find that John had taken another wife and

Harriet Tubman (far left) with six slaves she helped guide to freedom.
Courtesy of the Library of Congress.

Sojourner Truth

Among Tubman's contemporaries in the abolitionist movement was former slave, lecturer, and preacher Sojourner Truth (c. 1797–1883). Truth was born into slavery in Ulster County, New York, and given the name Isabella Baumfree. In 1826, just nine months before all slaves in New York were to be freed by a state law, Truth escaped from her master. Truth then filed a successful lawsuit for the return of her son, Peter. Peter had been sold to a wealthy farmer in Alabama in defiance of a New York law barring the out-of-state sale of slaves. Truth's victory in the courts, in an era when the legal system rarely worked in favor of former slaves or women, was truly exceptional.

In 1829 Truth moved to New York City and became involved with a religious commune that she later learned was headed by con artists. That experience, however, did not dampen Truth's religious convictions. In June 1843 Truth had a dream in which God told her to "Go East." She packed her bags and headed east into farm country. Along the way she changed her named to Sojourner Truth because she believed it was God's will that she "walk in truth." Truth adopted the lifestyle of a traveling preacher, giving sermons in churches, on street corners, at religious revivals, and in homes. Her sermons typically included antislavery themes. Truth, who stood six feet tall and had a commanding presence, rapidly gained a reputation as a provocative and inspirational speaker. She drew large crowds wherever she went.

In late 1843 Truth visited a cooperative farm called the Northhampton Association of Education and Industry. There she met several noted abolitionists,

was not interested in moving north. On her fourth rescue mission, Tubman helped eleven slaves, including one of her brothers and his wife, escape. She took them all the way to St. Catharines, Canada, a small town on the shores of Lake Ontario.

Earns nickname "Moses"

From 1852 to 1857 Tubman lived in St. Catharines. With a total population of six thousand, the town was home to seven hundred African Americans. During that period Tubman made eleven trips into Maryland. In the spring of 1857 she went on her most daring rescue. Traveling south by rail-

Sojourner Truth. *Courtesy of the Library of Congress.*

encouraged Truth to publish her memoirs and to become a speaker on the antislavery lecture circuit. Truth addressed women's rights conventions, abolitionist groups, and other gatherings, often bringing her audience to tears.

During the Civil War (1861–65) Truth supported African American soldiers by collecting food and clothing for them and caring for the wounded. In 1864 Truth was hired by the National Freedmen's Relief Association to assist newly freed slaves—many of whom were living in squalid refugee camps and slums. During the late 1860s Truth gave lectures that combined aspects of Christian religion, mysticism, feminism, and her passion for African American rights. Truth died at the age of eighty-six. Shortly before her death Truth told her family and friends, "I'm going home like a shooting star."

among them William Lloyd Garrison (1805–1879) and **Frederick Douglass** (1817–1895; see entry). The abolitionists

road during the daytime, Tubman went to Caroline County, Maryland, and rescued her elderly parents. She resettled her parents in Auburn, New York, in a house she purchased with assistance from her friend William Seward (1801–1872; governor of New York, U.S. senator, U.S. secretary of state).

Among both black and white abolitionists, Tubman's ceaseless work as an Underground Railroad conductor earned her the nickname "Moses." The name was a reference to the biblical Moses, who led the enslaved Hebrews out of captivity in Egypt to the promised land of Israel. Tubman was also well known to slave owners of the South. They posted a $40 thousand reward for her capture, dead or alive.

Civil War spy and scout

When the Civil War (1861–65) between the Confederacy (the South) and the Union (the North) broke out in April 1861, Tubman assisted the Union army. She first worked in a field hospital in Beaufort, South Carolina, caring for injured and wounded fugitive slaves and soldiers. In the summer of 1863—the year that President Lincoln issued the Emancipation Proclamation freeing the slaves—Tubman went to Charleston, South Carolina. There she served as a scout and a spy for an all-black Union regiment led by Colonel James Montgomery. The regiment's mission was to liberate slaves and carry out raids against rebel forces. As a spy, Tubman courageously gathered information from behind enemy lines—a skill she had sharpened during her years as a conductor on the Underground Railroad.

Abolitionist friends come to Tubman's support

In 1864 Tubman, penniless and exhausted, returned to her parent's home in Auburn, New York. Despite having served the Union army in many useful capacities, Tubman never received payment. After the war ended on April 9, 1865, Tubman traveled to Washington to try to secure a position as a paid nurse at a freedman's hospital in Virginia, and to see if she could collect her back pay from the army. She again went home empty-handed.

Tubman's abolitionist friends came to her aid with donations of money and clothing. Those donations enabled Tubman to support herself and her parents, as well as the many impoverished ex-slaves who showed up at her door. In 1869 Tubman's friend Sarah Bradford wrote a short biography of Tubman's life titled *Scenes in the Life of Harriet Tubman*. Proceeds from the sale of the book allowed Tubman to pay off the mortgage on her Auburn home.

In 1869 Tubman married Nelson Davis, a black Civil War veteran. Their marriage lasted nineteen years until Davis's death from tuberculosis.

Founds home for aged

In 1896, at age seventy-five, Tubman initiated a project to improve the quality of life for the poor and aged. Using the royalties from a second edition of Bradford's book, Tubman purchased twenty-five acres of land adjacent to her Auburn property and started a cooperative farm. She invited people of all ages to live and work there. Each person contributed according to his or her ability, and elderly and sick people were cared for there. Tubman served as manager, nurse, and cook of the cooperative until 1903. When she could no longer run the place by herself she donated the land to her church, the African Methodist Episcopal Zion Church.

The A.M.E. church formally opened the Harriet Tubman Home for Aged and Indigent Negroes in 1908. Tubman spent her remaining years peacefully at the home she had founded. She died in 1913 at age ninety-two and was buried with full military honors.

Sources

Books

Bentley, Judith. *Harriet Tubman.* New York: Franklin Watts, Inc., 1990.

Bradford, Sarah. *Harriet Tubman: The Moses of Her People.* New York: Corinth Press, 1961. Reprint of 1886 edition.

Burns, Bree. *Harriet Tubman and the Fight against Slavery.* New York: Chelsea House Publishers, 1992.

Logan, Rayford W., and Michael R. Winston, eds. *Dictionary of American Negro Biography.* New York: W. W. Norton & Co., 1982.

Mabee, Carleton. *Sojourner Truth: Slave, Prophet, Legend.* New York: New York University Press, 1993.

McClard, Megan. *Harriet Tubman: Slavery and the Underground Railroad.* Englewood, NJ: Silver Burdett Press, 1991.

McKissack, Patricia C., and Fredrick McKissack. *Sojourner Truth: Ain't I a Woman?* New York: Scholastic, Inc., 1992.

Sterling, Dorothy, ed. *We Are Your Sisters: Black Women in the Nineteenth Century.* New York: W. W. Norton & Co., 1984.

Ingrid Washinawatok

Born July 31, 1957
Keshena, Wisconsin
Died March 4, 1999
Colombia/Venezuela border (near La Victoria, Venezuela)

Native American activist

"Historically, we've been herded from one side of the country to the other by the U.S. Army. . . . we see toxic waste being poured into our rivers. We see our land base diminish. Our reservations have been battered. With each trauma that occurs, a piece of your heart is taken away."

Ingrid Washinawatok in Messengers of the Wind.

Ingrid Washinawatok.
Reproduced by permission of AP/Wide World Photos.

Ingrid Washinawatok was killed at the age of forty-one in Colombia by rebel soldiers. She had been in the South American nation assisting the U'wa Indians, who were attempting to prevent oil drilling on their land. Washinawatok's final humanitarian mission was representative of her life's work—struggling to keep alive native traditions and culture and to protect indigenous people's rights around the world. Washinawatok was executive director of the Fund of the Four Directions, cochair of the Women's Indigenous Network, and chair of the United Nations' Committee on the International Decade of the World's Indigenous Peoples.

Childhood on the reservation and in Chicago

Washinawatok was born on Menominee Indian Reservation in northeastern Wisconsin and grew up in Chicago, Illinois. Both of her parents were of the Menominee tribe. Her mother, Gwendolyn (Dodge) Washinawatok, worked as a registered nurse at the tribal hospital. Her father, James Washinawatok, served in the navy during World War II (1934–45), after which he attended college and earned degrees in political science and police administration. He then found work as an insurance claims adjuster in Chicago.

Washinawatok spent most of her childhood in Chicago, where she described her life as having been materially comfortable but emotionally isolating. "In school, I was on the outer fringes," stated Washinawatok. "Nobody wanted to play with me 'cause I didn't look like everybody else. Then I started making friends. I was supposed to know everything about Indians. Well, you get an American education, schools try to turn you into little white kids, but still you're supposed to know everything about Indians."

The family made frequent visits to the Menominee Reservation, where Washinawatok's grandfather lived on the Wolf River. "I'd sit in the backyard and just look up at the pines and evergreens against the blueness of the August sky," stated Washinawatok in *Messengers of the Wind*. When Washinawatok was a young girl, the tribal spiritual leader gave her the name O'Peqtaw Metamoh, which means "Flying Eagle Woman."

Activism begins at early age

When Washinawatok was an adolescent, her father was appointed a tribal judge and the family moved back to the Menominee Reservation (James Washinawatok later rose to the position of Menominee Nation Supreme Court justice). It was on the reservation that Washinawatok began fighting for the rights of her people. At the age of fourteen she worked with her father to protest environmental degradation and the sale of reservation land for tourism development. Throughout the 1970s Washinawatok participated in various Native American campaigns for tribal self-governance and sovereignty, civil rights for urban Native Americans, and the return of Native American lands.

After high school Washinawatok enrolled in the University of Wisconsin (UW). While a student, Washinawatok traveled to New York City to intern at the International Treaty Council, an organization that monitors indigenous (native) rights throughout the Americas. She left UW before completing her degree, because, in her words, "what I was learning didn't have much to do with the lives of Indian people." After

The Impact of U.S. Government Policy on the Menominee Tribe

The history of Washinawatok's people, the Menominees, is one of great injustice. Knowledge of that history influenced Washinawatok's decision to become a protector of Native American people and culture.

The name Menominee, Washinawatok explained in an interview published in the 1995 book *Messengers of the Wind,* means "the wild rice people." The original Menominee nation had occupied nine-and-a-half million acres in Wisconsin. The tribe's members had survived by hunting, fishing, and cultivating wild rice.

Washinawatok blamed federal legislation passed in 1934, called the Indian Reorganization Act (IRA), for having contributed to the decline of her tribe. The IRA stated that the U.S. government would recognize (and thus make assistance available to) tribal governments that operated by methods similar to the U.S. government—in the words of Washinawatok, a "corporate structure." Prior to that time, decisions affecting tribes had been made by consensus (unanimous agreement) of tribal members or councils of elders. The new bureaucratic form of government, Washinawatok argued, fostered corruption and encouraged leaders to take care of their own families at the expense of the rest of the tribe.

Another U.S. government policy that most historians now agree hurt the

that, Washinawatok went to work for the National Federation of Native Controlled Survival Schools.

In 1981 Washinawatok traveled to Geneva, Switzerland, to attend the Second International Non-Governmental Organization Conference on Indigenous People and the Land. The next year, at the age of twenty-five, Washinawatok married Ali El-Issa, a manager in a company that operates pharmacies. The couple had one son, born in 1985, named Maehki.

Cofounds Indigenous Women's Network

Washinawatok participated in the founding of the Indigenous Women's Network (IWN) in 1985, at the farm of activist **Janet McCloud** (1934- ; see entry) in Yelm, Washington. The IWN, in its promotional materials, defines itself as

Menominees and many other tribes was referred to as "termination" (passed in 1954). Under this policy, the U.S. government terminated (ended) the standing relationships, governed by treaties, between the United States and Indian tribes. Policymakers enacted termination in the hope that by voiding Native American treaty rights, Native Americans would be forced to assimilate (blend) into mainstream American society. Between 1954 and 1958 Congress terminated a total of 109 tribes, including the Menominees.

By the late 1950s the disastrous effects of termination had become clear. Native Americans from terminated tribes had plunged into poverty and many subsisted on welfare. Many Native Americans chose to leave their reservations and try living in cities. While health care had been free and housing and utilities subsidized on reservations, Native Americans who moved to cities were suddenly forced to foot the entire bill for rent, heat, and doctor's bills. "People felt so helpless because they couldn't provide for their families," stated Washinawatok, "and that's when a lot of them started drinking."

The last time tribes were terminated was in 1958, and the policy was officially revoked in 1970. In 1973 the Menominees became one of several nations to regain their tribal status, with full treaty rights.

working toward "the empowerment of Indigenous women, their families, communities, and Nations within the Americas and Pacific Basin."

Women from three hundred nations attended the five-day founding conference, which was dominated by discussions on alcoholism, domestic violence, child abuse, and other social ills plaguing Indian communities. The participants vowed to protect native lands, cultural practices, languages, and cultures. Washinawatok was named cochair of the IWN. She also became part of the editorial collective of the IWN's twice-yearly magazine *Indigenous Woman*.

Continues activism in New York City

As Washinawatok grew more interested in the struggles facing indigenous groups in Latin America, she learned Spanish.

She then moved to New York City and was hired by the International Indian Treaty Council to translate documents from Spanish to English. She found housing in Brooklyn, New York, where there was a sizable Native American community. Washinawatok also got to know the Shinnecock people and regularly attended powwows at their reservation on Eastern Long Island, New York.

Washinawatok's next position was with the Fund of the Four Directions, an organization that supports Native American culture. She started out as a program officer and worked her way up to executive director—the position she held at the time of her death. As executive director, Washinawatok determined the organization's policies regarding grant-making and began a program to revitalize indigenous languages.

In 1992 Washinawatok began serving on the board of directors of the American Indian Community House in Manhattan, New York. That organization provides activities for youths and elderly people, as well as health information, a day care center, and tribal dancing. Out of the Community House grew a nationally known theater troupe, called the Spider Women's Theater, that performs plays based on Native American experiences.

Addresses United Nations General Assembly

Throughout the 1990s Washinawatok served as chair of the United Nations' Committee on the International Decade of the World's Indigenous Peoples. In that position she traveled to dozens of countries to advocate for native people's rights. In December 1992 Washinawatok addressed the United Nations General Assembly, at a ceremony marking the start of the International Year of the World's Indigenous People. Like other indigenous leaders at the gathering, Washinawatok spoke out against the theft and environmental destruction of Indian lands and the need to retain indigenous cultures.

Washinawatok also worked with the Indigenous Initiative for Peace, an inter-American indigenous rights organization headed by Nobel Peace Prize laureate **Rigoberta Menchú** (1959– ; see entry).

Receives honors and awards

In 1998 Washinawatok was named Indian Woman of the Year by several indigenous rights organizations. That same year she was selected by the Rockefeller Foundation as an Outstanding Leader in the foundation's National Generation Leadership Program. And in 1998 the Northstar Foundation—a grant-making organization named in honor of the nighttime beacon slaves followed to freedom—gave Washinawatok its Outstanding Women prize.

Washinawatok has received many awards from organizations of African Americans, Asian Americans, and Hispanic Americans in recognition of her efforts on behalf of those communities.

Comes to assistance of U'Wa people

In early 1999 Washinawatok joined a delegation of indigenous-rights activists traveling to Colombia, South America. The purpose of the visit was to show solidarity with the U'Wa people—an indigenous group whose land was being threatened by oil exploration—and to help them develop a cultural education system for their children. The other members of the delegation were Terence Frietas, director of the U'Wa Defense Project, and Lahe'ena'e Gay, an Indian rights activist from Hawaii.

In 1992 the Colombian government, together with Occidental Petroleum (of the United States) and the Dutch and English branches of Shell Oil, announced plans to explore the mining of an estimated 1.5 billion barrels of oil beneath U'Wa land. The U'Wa people, who have lived in the cloud forest of the Colombian Andes for centuries, were vigorous in their opposition to the oil companies' intentions. In 1997 the five thousand U'Wa members threatened to commit mass suicide rather than witness the environmental destruction caused by oil drilling. The matter was tied up in Colombian courts for the next three years.

Frietas, a twenty-four-year-old biologist and passionate supporter of indigenous rights, became one of the few outsiders to gain the trust of the U'Wa people. In 1997 he brought U'Wa leader Roberto Cobaria to California to speak at an Occidental Petroleum shareholders meeting. The following year the U'Wa people invited Frietas to bring a delegation to their homeland.

Killed by Colombian rebel forces

On February 25, 1999, when Frietas, Cobaria, and Washinawatok were on their way to Bogotá (the capital of Colombia) to return home to the United States, they were abducted by masked men. Later identified as renegade soldiers of the Revolutionary Armed Forces of Colombia (FARC; the army that is trying to topple the Colombian government), the captors held Washinawatok and her companions hostage for one week before killing them. The trio's bullet-riddled bodies were discovered just across the Colombian border, in a field near La Victoria, Venezuela, on March 4, 1999. In a communiqué, FARC's commander stated that the killings had been ordered by a low-ranking officer without the consent of the FARC leadership and that the perpetrators would be punished. He asked forgiveness from the U'Wa people.

Memorial services for Washinawatok, held in both New York City and Keshena, Wisconsin, were attended by indigenous leaders from all over the world. "Her whole life was about humanity, about respecting people's ability to be who they are," stated Menominee Nation chairman Apesanahkwat in a *New York Times* article about Washinawatok's death.

"Ingrid touched the lives of many people who will remember her positive energy, charismatic personality and radiant enthusiasm to make the world a better place," stated an obituary in *Indian Country News*. "She made many friends . . . in her lifelong struggle to promote culture, traditions and human rights. . . . She was a dynamic warrior and an inspiration for Natives throughout the world. She will be remembered as a remarkable woman who served her people and others selflessly in life."

On May 15, 2000, the Superior Court of Bogotá (Columbia) ruled that Occidental Petroleum can drill for oil near U'Wa land. Members of the U'Wa nation pledged to intensify their opposition to the drilling.

Sources

Books

Katz, Jane, ed. *Messengers of the Wind: Native American Women Tell Their Life Stories*. New York: Ballantine Books, 1995, pp. 88–97.

Articles

"Colombia: Court Allows U.S. Oil Firm to Drill Near Indian Land." *The Ann Arbor News.* May 16, 2000: A3.

"Colombia Oil Exploration Turns Bloody." *Environmental News Network.* March 22, 1999.

Deer, Kenneth. "Ingrid Washinawatok Murdered in Colombia." *Eastern Door.* January 22, 1999.

Emblin, Richard. "No Rush to Justice." *Time.* April 19, 1999: 12.

Jacobs, Andrew. "Three Kidnapped Americans Killed; Colombian Rebels Are Suspected." *New York Times.* March 8, 1999: A1, A3.

Sachs, Susan. "Three Victims in Colombia Defended Indigenous People." *New York Times.* March 7, 1999: 18.

"Tribute to a Warrior Woman: Ingrid Washinawatok." *Contemporary Women's Issues.* Spring 1999: 1.

Wirpsa, Leslie. "U'wa Leader Defies Threat in Land Fight." *National Catholic Reporter.* October 31, 1997: 13.

Web Sites

"Friends and Relatives of the People: Ingrid Washinawatok, Terence Freitas, Lahe'ena'e Gay." [Online] Available http://www.alphacdc.com/ien/columbia.html (accessed March 1, 2000).

"O'Peqtaw-Metamoh (Flying Eagle Woman): Ingrid Washinawatok El-Issa." *News from Indian Country.* (March 21, 1999.) [Online] Available http://www.indiancountrynews.com/ingridobit.html (accessed March 1, 2000).

Two Shoes, Minnie. "Remembering Our Friend Ingrid." *News from Indian Country.* (March 21, 1999.) [Online] Available http://www.indiancountrynews.com/ingridminnie.html (accessed March 1, 2000).

Robert F. Williams

Born February 26, 1925
Monroe, North Carolina
Died October 15, 1996
Grand Rapids, Michigan

Civil rights activist and revolutionary

"Our people must stop allowing themselves to be beaten like common dogs in the streets. We will never receive protection until we return violence for violence."

Robert F. Williams in a broadcast of "Radio Free Dixie"

Robert F. Williams.
Reproduced by permission of Corbis Corporation (Bellevue).

In the late 1950s a different kind of civil rights movement was taking place in Monroe, North Carolina. In that town of six thousand, where the Ku Klux Klan (the Ku Klux Klan is an anti-black terrorist group formed in the South in the aftermath of the Civil War that has for decades intimidated and committed acts of violence against African Americans and members of other racial and ethnic minorities and religious groups) and the police rode roughshod over the African American community, the National Association for the Advancement of Colored People (NAACP) fought back with arms. Many members of that renegade NAACP branch were veterans of the armed forces. Their leader was Robert F. Williams.

Born to a family of black rights defenders

Robert Franklin Williams was born in Monroe, North Carolina, in 1925, to John L. Williams (a railroad boiler washer) and Emma C. Williams. Monroe, just fourteen miles from the border of South Carolina, was home to many former slaves—among them Robert's grandparents, Sikes Williams and Ellen Isabel Williams. Sikes Williams had been a Republican Party activist in the late 1800s (in the post-Civil War years, the Republican Party championed equal rights for African Americans) and the publisher of a newspaper called *The People's Voice*. Ellen Isabel Williams, whom Robert called his "greatest friend," was a prolific reader of history. Before Williams's grandmother died, she handed him the rifle that Sikes had used to fend off white terrorists at the turn of the century. Williams would keep that rifle for the rest of his life.

Williams had his first experience with the brutal nature of racism when he was ten years old. Then he witnessed a white policeman dragging an African American woman down the street by the ankle, with the woman's back scraping the pavement. White onlookers hooted and laughed while the woman screamed.

Works in Detroit and San Francisco

At the age of seventeen Williams left high school to seek training as a machinist. He then briefly attended an all-African American teachers college in Elizabeth City, North Carolina. In 1943 Williams moved to Detroit, Michigan, where he worked as a mill operator at the Ford Motor Company. At that time Williams became interested in the Communist Party—particularly in the organization's call for racial equality. (Communism is the theory of social organization based on the holding of all property in common.) He attended meetings and read the party's newspaper, although he did not become a party member.

Williams left Detroit later in 1943 after the outbreak of a race riot. Over a period of several days, mobs of white people terrorized African American residents and destroyed their property. Thirty-four African Americans died in the violence.

Williams next went to work at the Mare Island Navy Yard near San Francisco, California. Six months after starting that position, however, he quit due to the racial violence in employee dormitories.

Drafted into armed forces

Williams returned to Monroe, North Carolina, and shortly thereafter was drafted into the army. He was assigned to a Signal Corps battalion at Camp Crowder, Missouri, and began training as a telephone lineman. Following an illness, Williams was taken out of the training program and given a job as a typist. According to Williams, however, "the most important thing about the armed forces was that they taught us to use arms."

Williams served at a time when the armed forces were still segregated (separated by race; military segregation was ended in 1948). All-African American units were subjected to abuse by white officers. Williams stood up to the officers, for which he was imprisoned in the camp stockade. In 1946 Williams was honorably discharged (though not granted the customary "good conduct medal") and headed home to Monroe.

Organizes armed resistance to Klan

Soon after Williams's return to Monroe, another black veteran named Bennie Montgomery killed a white landowner named W. W. Mangum. Montgomery was a sharecropper on Mangum's land. He had cut Mangum's throat with a pocket knife after Mangum had slapped and kicked him. Montgomery was convicted of murder and executed for his crime. His remains were then returned to Monroe for burial by his family.

The local branch of the Ku Klux Klan announced its intention to intercept Montgomery's body and drag it through the streets of Monroe. Upon hearing the news, Williams and other local African American veterans organized an armed resistance to the Klan. On the appointed day Williams's group lined the street in front of the funeral parlor to which Montgomery's remains were to be delivered. The Klansmen arrived on the scene to find forty rifles trained upon them and drove away. The African American brigade had succeeded in its mission without firing a single shot.

Returns to school

From 1946 to 1952 Williams continued his education and worked at a variety of jobs. He began by earning his high school degree. At the same time he wrote poetry and prose and published a weekly column in the *Monroe Enquirer*. Williams then took advantage of the G.I. Bill (the law allowing members of the armed forces to receive a free college education) and enrolled in West Virginia State College. There he studied psychology and creative writing and wrote for the college newspaper. Williams next transferred to North Carolina College in Durham and took classes on literature.

In 1947 Williams married a woman named Mabel, also from Monroe. The couple eventually had three sons.

Receives combat training in marines

When Williams's G.I. benefits ran out in 1952, he went to work at the Curtis-Wright aircraft plant in New Jersey. Williams spent his spare time with white intellectual radicals from the American Labor Party.

As unemployment rose (especially in war-related industries), Williams found himself hired and fired from a succession of jobs. After traveling from coast to coast in search of work, he signed up with the marines.

Williams was assigned to Camp Pendleton, where he underwent special combat training. He was schooled in the use of machine guns, grenades, rocket launchers, and other weapons, and participated in mountain warfare training. Williams also spent 180 days in a military prison for refusing to salute the U.S. flag at a ceremony. He was discharged from the marines in 1955.

Rebuilds Monroe NAACP chapter

Williams returned home to Monroe at the age of thirty. He was optimistic that the nation was moving toward racial equality, as the year before had seen the landmark *Brown v. Board of Education* decision that outlawed segregated schools. Williams stepped up his own involvement in the civil rights movement, joining the predominantly white Unitarian Fellowship and the Monroe chapter of the National Association for the Advancement of Colored People (NAACP).

A year after Williams joined the NAACP, the group's membership shrank to six. Like other NAACP chapters throughout the South, Monroe's chapter was suffering from intimidation by the Ku Klux Klan. (As part of a backlash to the *Brown* decision and the victory of the Montgomery, Alabama, bus boycott [see entry on **Jo Ann Gibson Robinson**], the Klan was recruiting record numbers of members.) Klan rallies near Monroe drew upwards of fifteen thousand participants. In late 1956 the Monroe NAACP's remaining members decided to disband. When Williams objected, he was voted the group's president. Then everyone but Williams's friend, an African American veteran and physician named Albert E. Perry, quit the organization. Perry was named vice-president.

Williams and Perry rebuilt the group from the bottom up. They recruited members in pool halls and beauty parlors, and on street corners. They attracted domestic workers and unemployed people. They also brought into the fold many of the forty African American men who had faced down the Klan with guns a decade earlier. In contrast to other NAACP chapters, whose members were mostly middle-class professional African Americans and whites, the Monroe NAACP was a distinctly working-class outfit.

Undertakes desegregation campaigns

One of the Monroe NAACP's first campaigns was to desegregate the Union County Public Library. The mission was easily accomplished, with no resistance from the library's board of directors.

The next task proved much more difficult—that of desegregating Monroe's municipal swimming pool. The swimming pool was chosen because the African American community felt a pressing need for a safe place for their children to swim. Several African American children had drowned in backwoods swimming holes, drainage ditches, and ponds, even as blacks' tax dollars supported a pool for white children only. Williams led groups of African American youths to hold sit-ins (protests at a segregated facility in which participants refuse to leave) at the pool.

Takes up arms against the Klan again

While the sit-ins did not accomplish the desegregation of the pool, they did succeed in raising the ire of the Ku Klux Klan. The Klan staged numerous rallies, after which they drove their cars (in processions called motorcades) through Monroe's African American neighborhood—honking, shouting obscenities, and firing guns.

Local Klansmen determined that Williams and Perry were behind the pool desegregation campaign and attempted to drive the pair out of town. When Perry began receiving death threats, Williams recruited sixty NAACP members to form an armed militia. They obtained military surplus weapons and went into the woods for training. When the Klan targeted Perry's home for an attack following a rally in the summer of 1957, Williams's army was ready.

The African American militiamen erected a sandbag barrier in front of Perry's house, behind which they crouched with their weapons. The Klan motorcade of about eighty cars drove through the African American section of town. As they neared Perry's house, the NAACP members opened fire. "We shot it out with the Klan and repelled their attack," wrote Williams in *Negroes with Guns,* "and the Klan didn't have any more stomach for this type of fight. They stopped raiding our community." Soon thereafter, the Monroe city council passed an ordinance banning Klan motorcades.

Suspended from NAACP for vow to "meet violence with violence"

In 1958 and 1959 there were two legal cases that demonstrated the double standard of justice for African Americans and whites in Monroe. In the first case two African American youths were charged and nearly convicted of raping a white girl whom, in fact, they had only kissed on the cheek. Williams had been able to prevent the boys' conviction by enlisting the aid of famous New York defense lawyer Conrad Lynn. In the second case a white man was acquitted on charges of raping a young African American woman—even though the evidence clearly indicated his guilt.

Following the second verdict, in the spring of 1959, Williams addressed African American women and men assembled on the courthouse steps. "This demonstration today," he declared, "shows that the Negro in the South cannot expect justice in the courts. He must convict his attackers on the spot. He must meet violence with violence, lynching with lynching." (Lynching is the extralegal execution of a person, usually an African American, accused of a crime or a violation of social mores, often by hanging, by a group of three or more people.)

Williams's statement was widely reported in the press. The next day NAACP executive director Roy Wilkins suspended Williams from the NAACP for six months. Williams's wife served as Monroe NAACP president in his absence, and Williams was unanimously reelected to the position at the end of the six months. During his suspension, Williams began publishing a newspaper dedicated to African American liberation called *The Crusader.*

Charged with kidnapping white couple

Racial tensions heated up in August of 1959 when a group of Freedom Riders arrived in Monroe. (Freedom Rides were journeys throughout the South by integrated groups of people attempting to desegregate public transportation facilities). The African American and white Freedom Riders joined local African Americans—led by Williams—in a picket at the courthouse demanding desegregation of facilities and equal employment opportunities. Klansmen, aided by the police, beat the picketers.

Williams, after having received several death threats, stationed armed African American guards along his street and outside his house. One evening in late August, following a confrontation between civil rights activists and a white mob at the courthouse, a white couple named the Steagalls drove onto Williams's street. Their car was recognized as one that the previous day had sported a racist banner proclaiming "Open Season on Coons" (meaning it was time for killing African Americans). The car was surrounded by armed African Americans, who cried "Kill them, kill them!" Williams, fearing for the white couple's lives, escorted them into the safety of his home. Although Williams explained his intentions to the Steagalls, Mrs. Steagall repeatedly shouted that she and her husband had been kidnapped. Williams recognized that such a charge would lead to his arrest. He gathered his wife and children and headed out of town.

Exile in Cuba and China

Williams spent the next eight years in exile. First he and his family moved to Cuba because, as he explained in *Negroes with Guns,* "I could think of no other place in the Western Hemisphere than Cuba where a Negro would be treated as a human being; where the race problem would be understood." Williams was warmly welcomed by Cuban president Fidel Castro (1927–; see box in Ernesto "Ché" Guevara entry) and revolutionary hero **Ernesto "Ché" Guevara** (1928–1967; see entry).

Williams was given access to a radio station in the capital city of Havana. From 11 P.M. to midnight every Friday he broadcast "Radio Free Dixie," which could be heard all across the United States. Williams also continued to publish *The Cru-*

Williams's Death Sparks Fresh Look at Civil Rights Movement

One only has to look at the life of Robert F. Williams to realize that the civil rights movement was not limited to nonviolent action. Few history books acknowledge that African Americans, in their quest for freedom, used a variety of tactics—including violence—to respond to the injustice around them.

Author Timothy B. Tyson reflected on the armed struggle in Monroe, and its place within the broader civil rights movement, in a December 1997 article in the NAACP's newsletter, *The Crisis*. "The struggle in Monroe finds no place in our cinematic confections of the civil rights movement," wrote Tyson. "Robert Williams eludes our recollection because in our memories we have polished the movement smooth, grinding off its rougher edges and grittier realities, forgetting how we won and lost and at what bitter cost.

"The fact that Rosa Parks had to remind us to remember Robert Williams reflects our distorted memory of the freedom movement. Film images of peaceful marchers facing police dogs and fire hoses remain the most enduring—and most inspiring—of the era. But living in tension and in tandem with nonviolent direct action were those willing to defend home and community by armed force if necessary. By remembering only the powerful oratory of Dr. King and the patient litigation of the NAACP, we overlook the brutality of the world they sought to change and even understate the magnitude of their achievements."

sader, which then had a circulation of forty thousand. The paper was distributed by civil rights organizers in the South.

Williams visited North Vietnam in 1964, during the Vietnam War (1954–75). There he met North Vietnamese leader Ho Chi Minh and wrote articles about racism and war for distribution to African American soldiers. Williams moved with his family to China in 1965. They spent two years there as guests of Chinese leader Mao Tse-tung (1893–1976).

During his years abroad Williams kept in close touch with radical African American activists. He even helped found the Republic of New Africa (RNA), a revolutionary organization dedicated to establishing a separate black nation within five of the southern states in the United States. Williams was made the RNA's president-in-exile.

Returns to United States

By 1969 Williams longed for home. Although he had lived comfortably in Cuba and China, he believed his place was in the United States, fighting for his people. That September he flew to Detroit and turned himself in at the federal building. He was released on $11,000 bond, after which he settled in the small fishing community of Baldwin, in western Michigan. In 1976 Williams received word that the kidnapping charge against him had been dropped.

Williams spent the next twenty-seven years lecturing and writing about civil rights. He also founded the People's Association for Human Rights in his new hometown and worked with the Lake/Newaygo branch of the NAACP. In 1992 he was awarded that branch's Black Image Award. He added that honor to the Outstanding Contributions prize he had received from the Association of Black Social Workers in 1987.

Williams died from complications of Hodgkin's disease on October 15, 1996, in Grand Rapids, Michigan. He was seventy-one years old. Rosa Parks was among the dignitaries at Williams's funeral, held in Monroe, North Carolina. Parks lauded Williams "for his courage and his commitment to freedom."

"The work that he did should go down in history and never be forgotten," declared Parks.

Sources

Books

Cohen, Robert Carl. *Black Crusader: A Biography of Robert Franklin Williams.* Seacaucus, NJ: Lyle Stuart, Inc., 1972.

Tyson, Timothy B. *Radio Free Dixie: Robert F. Williams and the Roots of Black power.* Chapel Hill: University of North Carolina Press, 1999.

Williams, Robert F. *Negroes with Guns.* Reprint ed. Detroit: Wayne State University Press, 1998.

Articles

Stout, David. "Robert F. Williams, 71, Civil Rights Leader and Revolutionary." (Obituary.) *New York Times.* October 19, 1996.

Tyson, Timothy B. "Robert F. Williams, NAACP: Warrior and Rebel." *The Crisis.* December 1997–January 1998: 14–18.

"Where Are They Now? Uncompromising Radical." *Newsweek.* August 3, 1970: 8.

Harry Wu

Born February 8, 1937
Shanghai, China

Human rights activist

After nineteen years as a prisoner in China's notorious system of labor camps, Harry Wu emerged as the camps' most vocal critic. Wu moved to the United States and brought to light the fact that many Chinese exports are produced by forced labor in prisons. He has returned to his native land four times to document ongoing abuses in labor camps, using hidden cameras. On Wu's most recent trip, in 1995, he was detained for two months and convicted of spying before being expelled to the United States.

Wealthy beginnings in Shanghai

Wu was born Wu Hongda (Harry was a nickname given him in school) in Shanghai, China, in 1937. His father was a banker, and the family lived a very comfortable existence in their three-story, art-filled home. Wu's mother died when Wu was five years old, and his father remarried the next year. The third child of eight, Wu went to schools run by Roman Catholic Jesuit missionaries.

In 1949 China underwent a communist revolution. (Communism is the theory of social organization based on the

"The United States wants market access to China, imagining every Chinese drinking ten cans of Coca-Cola a day. But human rights receives only lip service while the U.S. acts primarily on trade deals."

Harry Wu in a January 2000 interview.

Harry Wu.
Reproduced by permission of AP/Wide World Photos.

583

holding of all property in common, overseen by a centralized government.) Communist Party chairman Mao Tse-tung (1893–1976) took power and initiated sweeping reforms. While the new system of government improved the standard of living of some of China's poorest citizens, it was financially damaging to many wealthy Chinese families—like the Wus. Rather than leave the country, however, Harry's father decided to stay in China and help with the nation's reconstruction.

Political difficulties begin in college

After completing his secondary studies, Wu enrolled in the Beijing Geology Institute in Beijing, China. The university had been established by Communist Party officials interested in learning how to better locate and mine China's vast underground natural resources. In addition to offering a science curriculum, the institute was a training ground for future Communist Party members. Wu, however, resisted pressure to join the party's Youth League. His interests were limited to his studies, playing on the baseball team, and planning a future with his girlfriend in Shanghai.

In 1957 the Communist Party announced its "Let a Thousand Flowers Bloom" campaign, in which it encouraged citizens to offer frank feedback about governmental policies. Wu attended a campaign meeting, at which he voiced criticisms about the government and about leaders of the Youth League.

Denounced as a counterrevolutionary

As it turned out, the party was not sincere in its request for open dialogue, and Wu paid heavily for his honesty. He was denounced at a Youth League meeting for his "poisonous ideas" and accused of opposing communism—or, in official language, being a "counterrevolutionary rightist." Wu was shunned by his classmates and his friends on the baseball team. Even his girlfriend deserted him. For his final two years of college, Wu was constantly guarded by Youth League members and prohibited from leaving the campus.

"The Party might disagree with my views, I thought," Wu wrote in his memoir, *Bitter Winds,* "but I had never done anything wrong or committed any crime. I certainly did not see myself as an enemy of the socialist system, and I didn't understand how they could brand me with the severest political label. I still sincerely wanted to work hard for my country, and it seemed preposterous to consider me an 'enemy of the people.'"

Imprisoned for opposing government

On April 27, 1960—just weeks before he was to graduate—Wu was denounced for his views and arrested. He was sentenced to "reeducation through labor" and taken to a detention center. There he wrote his family, informing them of his arrest. Wu's stepmother killed herself upon receipt of Wu's letter.

Wu spent several weeks at the detention center, awaiting his reassignment to a labor camp (he never had a trial). The detention center was overcrowded. Men slept side by side, each one allotted a space just two feet wide, on a brick platform. Food was scarce; prisoners barely subsisted on small, dark, bitter buns made of sorghum and wheat chaff, and watery soup. Wu and other prisoners were made to attend daily political reeducation classes, during which they had to admit the error of their antirevolutionary beliefs.

Political offenders like Wu were placed in the same facility as thieves and beggars. For the first time, Wu came in contact with peasants and other members of the lower classes—people who made up some 80 percent of China's population but from whom Wu had been shielded by his privileged upbringing. From streetwise jailmates, Wu learned the skills necessary to survive in prison, such as stealing food and fighting.

Nightmarish conditions in the laogai

Wu's program of "reeducation through labor" lasted nineteen years. (For an extensive account of Wu's imprisonment, see Wu's 1994 book *Bitter Winds: A Memoir of My Years in China's Gulag*.) During that time he was transferred among twelve different labor camps. (China's forced labor camp system—the world's largest—is referred to in Chinese as *laogai*.) Conditions in the camps were horrible: prisoners had to work long hours at hard, dangerous tasks. They were fed very little. Many prisoners died of malnutrition, disease, or starvation; Wu's own weight dropped to 72 pounds. At various points in his incarceration, he broke his arm, leg, and back in work-related accidents.

In the fall of 1961 Wu was near death. He was transferred to a unit for prisoners too weak to walk. From his bed he watched men die and their corpses removed daily. When Wu's friend Chen Ming died Wu accompanied Ming's corpse to the burial ground. On the way back to the barracks, Wu had "what seemed almost a revelation."

"Human life has no value here, I thought bitterly," wrote Wu in *Bitter Winds*. "But if a person's life has no value, then the society that shapes that life has no value either. If the people mean no more than dust, then the society should not continue, then I should oppose it.

"At that moment I knew that I could not die. . . . I had to use my life purposefully and try to change the society."

Conditions improve slightly

Wu was sent to work in a mine in 1969. Although he was still held captive, his status was altered to "resettlement worker," and restrictions upon him were slightly relaxed. He was even allowed to marry; he wed a woman named Shen Jiarui who, like himself, was a resettlement worker. The couple made their home in an abandoned cave outside the mine compound. They made no attempt to escape, as their capture would have resulted in torture or execution.

In 1974 Wu was granted permission to visit his family in Shanghai. It was his first time home in seventeen years.

Released from prison; travels to United States

In 1979, with the help of a police captain whom Wu had befriended, Wu was released. Wu was assigned to a teaching position, yet he felt it would be impossible to ever live freely in his own country. At the urging of his father, Wu applied for a passport and made plans to join his older sister in the United States. It was difficult for Wu, being a former political prisoner, to obtain permission to leave the country. When Wu found out that his wife was secretly working to derail his passport application, he divorced her.

In 1985 Wu finally obtained the necessary paperwork and left China. He arrived in California with forty dollars in his pocket and the offer of a teaching position at the University of California-Berkeley. He began the process of becoming a United States citizen.

Publicizes abuses in China's prison system

Wu strove to achieve a degree of normalcy in his life as a scholar of geology, yet he was unable to shake the vivid memories of his past. He decided to work to change the repression in his homeland, rather than try to forget about it. In 1988 Wu obtained a fellowship at Stanford University's Hoover Institution on War, Revolution, and Peace in Stanford, California, and began his study of China's laogai system.

Wu discovered that prison labor—in violation of international law—was being used to manufacture products in Chinese factories that were then being exported to the United States. To better understand the implications of human rights abuses in Chinese production of consumer goods, Wu studied the export trade business and the history of U.S.-China business relations.

In 1992 Wu established the Laogai Foundation to educate Americans about human rights abuses in China and to advocate for reform. That same year he published his first book about the labor camps, titled *Laogai: The Chinese Gulag*.

Tapes secret footage for *60 Minutes*

In 1991 Wu made his first of four trips to China to document ongoing abuses in prison camps. On that trip, Wu, accompanied by his new wife (a Taiwanese American named Ching-Lee Chen), entered the country using his American passport. Wu and Chen managed to visit twenty prison camps by posing as tourists or foreign business people. Chen took video footage with a camera hidden in her handbag, which had been provided by the CBS news show *60 Minutes*. Wu documented that products made at prison factories were subsequently relabeled with the name of a civilian factory. In that way, importers could not know that the goods had been produced by forced labor.

60 Minutes aired the footage collected by Wu and Chen in 1991, setting off a debate in Congress on U.S.-China relations. Wu testified before a congressional committee in September 1991, urging the United States to use its tremendous economic power to make China institute reforms.

Makes two more fact-finding trips

Wu returned to China twice over the next three years, each time gathering additional information about the prison camps. At times Wu even wore a policeman's uniform to avoid detection. On one visit Wu carried a hidden camera belonging to the British Broadcasting Corporation (BBC). The footage he captured was used in two subsequent documentaries on China's laogai system. In one of the programs Wu exposed evidence that the Chinese government was selling organs of executed prisoners to wealthy Chinese and foreigners.

Wu learned that since 1949 more than fifty million million people have been held prisoner in China's labor camp system and that China profits off this massive incarceration by selling hundreds of millions of dollars worth of prisoner-produced goods to the West. Wu's revelations have resulted in closer inspection of Chinese imports and the rejection of numerous shipments of products of suspicious origin. So far, however, he has been unable to get the United States to cut off trade with China pending China's improvement of human rights.

Arrested on fourth trip to China

On June 19, 1995, Wu once again traveled to his homeland. That time, however, Chinese officials at the border with Kazakhstan found Wu's name on a list of "undesirables" and arrested him. Wu was placed in detention and not allowed to contact the U.S. Embassy (the standard procedure for U.S. citizens) for over three weeks.

After sixty-six days in detention, during which time there was significant international outcry for his release, Wu was brought to trial. He was charged with spying, found guilty, and sentenced to fifteen years in prison. He was then ordered out of the country. The trial, it turned out, had been merely for show since Wu's release to the custody of U.S. officials had been prearranged.

Wu's arrest, fortunately for him, had just preceded a planned visit by first lady Hillary Rodham-Clinton (wife of U.S.

president Bill Clinton) to Beijing for a United Nations World Conference on Women. If Wu had remained in prison, Hillary Clinton would have boycotted the meeting, and the Chinese government would have faced censure by the international community.

Resumes human rights work

Wu returned to the United States to continue writing, lecturing, researching, and giving testimony before Congress. In 1996 he published *Troublemaker: One Man's Crusade against China's Cruelty,* describing his fact-finding trips to China. Wu also produced a documentary for television titled *Chinese Prison Labor: Inside China's Gulag,* featuring his secretly recorded video footage. In 1997 alone Wu logged two hundred speaking engagements.

Wu was asked in a January 2000 interview what types of reforms he would like to see in China. "Allow **Amnesty International** (AI; see entry) to operate its office in China," he responded. "No big deal. Allow the Red Cross International to go into the Chinese labor camps. Allow individuals to set up television stations, publish books. Allow the workers to organize their own unions. These are simple tests for human rights. These are the sorts of things we want to see for China."

Wu's Public Message Unsealed

Before his first return to China in 1991, Wu placed a note in a sealed envelope. He handed it to friends in the United States with instructions that it was only to be opened in the event that he was imprisoned. In June 1995, following Wu's arrest by Chinese authorities at the border, Wu's friends opened the envelope. The enclosed message, which was printed in the *New Yorker* that July, read as follows:

> Returning to the mainland holds great dangers for me, not the least of which is the possibility of once more losing the freedom and happiness that were so hard to come by in the first place and of causing my beloved wife to endure a lifetime of sadness and pain. But, still, the sound from the mine in my ears seems to ask, 'Who will go?' And the answer that comes back is: 'If I don't go, then who will?'

Sources

Books

Perkins, Dorothy. *Encyclopedia of China: The Essential Reference to China, Its History and Culture.* New York: Facts on File, Inc., 1999, pp. 575.

Wu, Harry. *Bitter Winds: A Memoir of My Years in China's Gulag.* New York: John Wiley and Sons, Inc., 1994.

Wu, Harry. *Laogai: The Chinese Gulag*. Boulder, CO: Westview Press, 1992.

Wu, Harry. *Troublemaker: One Man's Crusade against China's Cruelty*. New York: Times Books, 1996.

Articles

Goode, Stephen. "Wu Decries U.S. Denial of Chinese Crackdown." *Insight on the News*. January 24, 2000: 37.

Sciolino, Elaine. "China's Prisons Forged Zeal of U.S. Crusader." *New York Times*. July 10, 1995: A1.

Southerland, Daniel. "The Witness against China: Ex-Prisoner Harry Wu Shakes Up China Debate." *Washington Post*. September 29, 1991: H1.

Walder, Joyce. "Public Lives: Witness to the Atrocity Behind the Medicine." *New York Times*. February 27, 1998: B2.

Emiliano Zapata

Born August 8, 1879
Anenecuilco, Morelos, Mexico
Died April 10, 1919
Hacienda Chinameca, Morelos, Mexico

Rebel leader and land reform advocate

The actions of Emiliano Zapata were driven by one powerful desire: to see lands, stolen from peasant farmers by wealthy agriculturalists, returned to their rightful owners. To that end, Zapata first sought relief through legal channels. When that failed he resorted to taking up arms.

With a guerrilla army that varied in size from fifteen hundred to twenty thousand men, Zapata waged a nine-year-long war against a series of corrupt Mexican government leaders. Zapata seized plantation lands and turned them over to peasants. At the height of his power, Zapata controlled about one-third of Mexico. Zapata remains a folk hero among Mexico's agricultural laborers.

Experiences loss of family's lands

Although there is some uncertainty as to Emiliano Zapata's exact birth date (estimates range between 1873 and 1883), the most commonly accepted is August 8, 1879. Zapata was born in a farming village of four hundred people called Anenecuilco, in the Mexican state of Morelos (south of Mexico

"The land belongs to those who work it."

Emiliano Zapata

Emiliano Zapata.
Reproduced by permission of Corbis Corporation (Bellevue).

591

City). He grew up in relative comfort; his family owned land and livestock, which spared them the poverty, misery, and hard manual labor that characterized the lives of most of the other villagers. Nonetheless, from an early age Zapata sympathized with the plight of his neighbors.

During the few years that Zapata attended elementary school, he witnessed the illegal seizure of his neighbors' farms by sugar plantation owners—with the backing of corrupt politicians. Many of those left without land were forced to work as day laborers, sometimes on the land they used to own. In 1887 Zapata's family lost their orchards to greedy plantation owners. Legend has it that the young Emiliano responded to the theft of his family's lands by stating, "When I am big I will make them return them."

Zapata's parents died when he was sixteen years old, leaving him to care for his two sisters (he had an older brother who had moved out of the area). Zapata made his living by growing watermelons and raising mules.

Becomes president of village council

At the age of seventeen Zapata began participating in delegations of Anenecuilco men who protested the theft of their land. Zapata gained a reputation for boldly standing up to those in power. His involvement in the struggle intensified and he eventually became leader of the village's legal campaign for redress.

In 1909, when Zapata was thirty years old, he was elected president of the village council. Part of Zapata's job was to safeguard the land titles that served as a record of the villagers' land ownership. It was expected that one day the lands would be reclaimed, and the papers would ensure the lands were returned to their rightful owners.

With no legal relief in sight, in 1910 Zapata initiated a campaign to forcibly retake the stolen lands. He and his men encountered little opposition from the surprised plantation owners.

Mexican Revolution begins

While Zapata was busy recovering lands in Anenecuilco, a serious challenge was being mounted to the rule of dictator

Porfirio Díaz. Díaz (1830–1915) had been in power since 1876, except for the years 1880–1884. Under his rule a tiny proportion of Mexicans controlled a tremendous amount of wealth while the majority of the population lived in poverty. Díaz's challenger was a reformer named Francisco Madero. Díaz had Madero arrested and exiled to Texas. From across the border Madero called upon Mexicans to rise up against the government on November 20, 1910. November 20, however, passed uneventfully.

It was not until Madero returned to Mexico in February 1911 that the Mexican Revolution got underway. Zapata proclaimed his support for Madero, based on Madero's promise of instituting land reform. Zapata organized a band of guerrilla fighters (small groups who wage surprise attacks) from his home region and wrested control of towns and plantations throughout eastern Morelos.

Zapata was rapidly recognized as a skillful military leader and was made commander of several columns of rebels. He led 1,500 men north through Morelos, launching surprise attacks against military installations. His forces won a series of military victories, contributing to Díaz's decision of to flee the country on May 31, 1911.

Challenges the Madero government

Zapata's support for Madero did not last long, however, for once in power Madero revealed that he would not support the return of plantation lands to the peasants. Zapata then kept on fighting, with the goal of overthrowing Madero. Revolutionary forces led by Pancho Villa (1877–1923) took up arms in the north of Mexico, forcing Madero to divide his soldiers between the two fronts.

Madero called Zapata a "bandit" and instituted martial law throughout the land. Madero's insult prompted Zapata to draft a political platform, which Zapata called the Plan de Alaya (pronounced plahn day ahl-EYE-ah; see box).

Zapata's forces continued advancing through Morelos. As they went, they occupied plantations, evicted the owners, and distributed the lands to local peasants. Zapata's army even established a Rural Loan Bank to provide credit to peasants who received land so they could purchase seeds and equipment for planting.

The Plan de Alaya

On November 25, 1911, Zapata issued his revolutionary manifesto called the Plan de Alaya. It advocated the overthrow of Madero's government, the forcible repossession of lands stolen from farmers, and the redistribution of one-third of all plantation lands to peasants. The plan was coauthored by Zapata and Otilio Montaño, a schoolteacher in Villa de Ayala, and was published in a Mexico City newspaper. Zapata's plan earned him many new supporters.

"The immense majority of the common people and citizens of Mexico," read the Plan, "own no more than the land upon which they walk, suffering the horrors of miserable poverty without being able to better their social condition in any way nor to dedicate themselves to industry of agriculture because the lands, timber, and water are monopolized in a few hands."

Joins forces with Villa

In February 1913 President Madero was killed in a mutiny by the armed forces, and General Victoriano Huerta proclaimed himself the next president. For Zapata the change in leadership meant little; Huerta was no more a supporter of land reform than Madero had been.

Zapata's forces continued advancing northward toward Mexico City. They were joined in their fight by rebel groups led by Madero supporters Venustiano Carranza and Alvaro Obregón, as well as Pancho Villa's army. By August 1914 Huerta had been driven out of Mexico and Carranza had taken over as president.

Carranza aimed to unify the rebel forces behind his rule and to bring an end to the fighting. Zapata made his allegiance to Carranza conditional on Carranza's support of the Plan de Alaya; Carranza refused to endorse the plan. Other revolutionary leaders rejected Carranza's power grab and demanded that elections be held.

In the meantime, Zapata's forces approached Mexico City from the south and Villa's forces from the north. In November 1914 Zapata's forces overtook the capital, and Carranza's forces retreated to Veracruz province. The next month Villa joined Zapata in Mexico City and the two leaders formed an alliance. Zapata, who was anxious to return to his campaign of land reclamation in Morelos, left the occupation of the capital to Villa's forces.

Revolutionary forces face defeats

Villa's army was defeated in the first half of 1915. From that point on, Carranza devoted all his military strength to the battle against Zapata. Zapata's forces were put on the defen-

Pancho Villa and Zapato with their army of peasants during the Mexican Revolutionary War.
Reproduced by permission of Archive Photos.

sive; by the end of 1916 Zapata's manpower had been reduced from twenty thousand to five thousand. Carranza consolidated his hold on the capital and at times even took control of Morelos. Zapata's soldiers grew weary of fighting and mutinies broke out. Carranza's forces attacked Morelos in 1918, and a military stalemate ensued.

The end for Zapata came on April 10, 1919, when he was lured into a trap by a former Carranza general who claimed he wished to defect to Zapata's side. As Zapata walked past a line of the general's guards at the Hacienda Chinameca (a hacienda is a plantation), the guards raised their hands in salute. One of the guards then shot Zapata twice at point-blank range. Zapata died on the spot. Even though Zapata's body was placed on public display, many of his supporters refused to believe he was dead.

In 1994 a guerrilla peasant army calling themselves the Zapatistas staged an uprising in the state of Chiapas, again raising the issue of land reform.

Sources

Books

Button, John. *The Radicalism Handbook: A Complete Guide to the Radical Movement in the Twentieth Century.* London, England: Cassell, 1995.

"Emiliano Zapata." In *Dictionary of Hispanic Biography.* Detroit: Gale Research, Inc., 1996.

Ragan, John David. *Emiliano Zapata.* New York: Chelsea House Publishers, 1989.

Southerland, James E. "Emiliano Zapata." In *Dictionary of World Biography; The 20th Century.* Vol. 9. Edited by Frank N. Magill. Chicago: Fitzroy Dearborn Publishers, 1999, pp. 4104–4117.

Womack, John, Jr. *Zapata and the Mexican Revolution.* New York: Alfred A. Knopf, 1969.

Web Sites

"Emiliano Zapata." DISCovering Biography. The Gale Group. [Online] Available http://galenet.gale.com (accessed April 20, 2000).

Index

Illustrations are
marked by (ill.).

Black Creek Village *2:* 209.
	See also Love Canal
Black Expo *2:* 279
Black Hills, South Dakota
	1: 34–35
Black Panther Party *1:* 39, 63,
	72–79, 131–32; *2:* 349
Black Panther, The 1: 73
Black Power movement *1:* 130
Black Power (poster) *1:* 74 (ill.)
Black Skin, White Masks 1: 175
Blackwell, Unita *1:* 80 (ill.),
	80–87
*Blackwell v. Issaquena County
	Board of Education 1:* 85
"Bloody Sunday," *2:* 310–11
*Blues Legacies and Black Feminism:
	Gertrude "Ma" Rainey, Bessie
	Smith, and Billie Holiday
	1:* 133
Bolsheviks *3:* 454
Bombing *1:* 130
"Bombingham," *3:* 510
Borneo *3:* 411–12
Botha, P. W. *2:* 342, 356
Brightman, Lehman "Lee," *1:* 3
British Broadcasting Corporation
	(BBC) *3:* 588
Brotherhood of Sleeping Car
	Porters (BSCP) *3:* 443
Brown, Elaine *1:* 79
Brown, John *1:* 88 (ill.),
	88–95, 156
Brown v. Board of Education 577
Bryant, Louise *3:* 453–54
BSCP. *See* Brotherhood of Sleeping
	Car Porters (BSCP)
Bureau of Indian Affairs (BIA)
	1: 36
Burgos-Debray, Elizabeth *2:* 390
Burma *3:* 540
*Burma and India: Some Aspects of
	Intellectual Life under
	Colonialism 3:* 541
Burns, Lucy *3:* 429
Burnum, Burnum *3:* 414–15,
	415 (ill.)
Bus boycotts *2:* 246–47, 306–7;
	3: 447, 478–81
Bush, George *3:* 486
BYNC. *See* Back of the Yards
	Neighborhood Council
	(BYNC)

C

California Proposition 187 *3:* 504
California Proposition 209 *3:* 504
CAM. *See* Catholic Action
	Movement (CAM)
Cambridge, Battle of *3:* 464
Cambridge, Maryland *3:* 458
Cambridge, Treaty of *3:* 462–63
Camp David Accords *2:* 324
"Campaign to End Slums," *2:* 311
Canada *3:* 561
CAP. *See* Chicago Area Project
	(CAP)
Capital 2: 376
Capone, Al *1:* 11
Carl von Ossietzky Medal for
	Courage *1:* 125
Carmichael, Stokely *3:* 529 (ill.)
Carranza, Venustiano *3:* 594
Carter, Amy *2:* 266
Carter, Jimmy *2:* 207, 265, 324;
	3: 486
Caste system *2:* 197
Castro, Fidel *1:* 145; *2:* 230–33,
	233 (ill.); *3:* 437, 580
Castro, Raul *2:* 230
Catholic Action Movement
	(CAM) *1:* 180
Catholic Church *1:* 122. *See also*
	Irish Republican Army
Catholic Peace Fellowship *1:* 67
Catholic Worker 1: 138–39
Catholic Worker communal
	farms *1:* 139
Catholic Worker houses *1:* 139
Catholic Worker movement
	1: 141
CBNS. *See* Center for the Biology
	of Natural Systems (CBNS)
CCHW. *See* Citizen's
	Clearinghouse for Hazardous
	Waste (CCHW)
Center for Health, Environment,
	and Justice (CHEJ) *2:* 210
Center for Study of Responsive
	Law (CSRL) *3:* 400
Center for the Biology of
	Natural Systems (CBNS)
	1: 115–16, 119
Central Committee of the
	Communist League *2:* 375
Central Intelligence Agency (CIA)
	1: 22; *2:* 229, 233; *3:* 424, 497

N

NAACP. *See* National Association for the Advancement of Colored People (NAACP)

NAAPID. *See* National African American Parent Involvement Day (NAAPID)

Nader, Ralph *2:* 320; *3:* 395 (ill.), **395–402,** 398 (ill.)

Naders Raiders *3:* 398 (ill.), 399–400

NAFTA. *See* North American Free Trade Agreement (NAFTA)

Naidu, Sorojini *2:* 199 (ill.)

NALC. *See* Negro American Labor Council (NALC)

Narrative of the Life of Frederick Douglass 1: 154–55

Nashville Student Movement *3:* 526

Nasrin, Taslima *3:* 403 (ill.), **403–10**

Nation of Islam (NOI) *2:* 345–48

National African American Parent Involvement Day (NAAPID) *1:* 164

National American Woman Suffrage Association (NAWSA) *1:* 5; *3:* 428, 521

National Association for the Advancement of Colored People (NAACP) *1:* 5, 49, 53, 159; *2:* 246, 260; *3:* 448, 479, 508, 524, 555, 577

National Black Women's Health Project *1:* 134

National Coalition on Racism in Sports and Media (NCRSM) *3:* 554

National Conference of Black Mayors (NCBM) *1:* 80, 86

National Conference of Social Work *1:* 5

National Congress of American Indians *3:* 555

National Consumers' League (NCL) *2:* 303

National Council of Negro Women *1:* 85; *3:* 464

National Farm Workers Association (NFWA) *1:* 98

National Federation of Charities and Corrections *1:* 5

National Guard *3:* 461–62

National League for Democracy (NLD) *3:* 543

National Opposition Union (UNO) *3:* 497

National Organization for Women (NOW) *2:* 271–72, 274 (ill.), 275; *3:* 555

National Political Caucus of Black Women *1:* 134

National Science Foundation *1:* 114

National Traffic and Motor Vehicle Safety Act (1966) *3:* 398

National Urban League *1:* 51; *3:* 448

National Woman's Party (NWP) *3:* 429

National Women's Hall of Fame *1:* 117

Nationalism *2:* 334

Native American fishing rights *1:* 31; *2:* 380–81

NAWSA. *See* National American Woman Suffrage Association (NAWSA)

Nazi Party *1:* 28

NCBM. *See* National Conference of Black Mayors (NCBM)

NCL. *See* National Consumers' League (NCL)

NCRSM. *See* National Coalition on Racism in Sports and Media (NCRSM)

Negro American Labor Council (NALC) *3:* 445, 448

Negt, Oskar *1:* 130

Nehrum, Jawaharial *3:* 469

Neighborhood Guild *1:* 4

Neighborhood Service Organization *1:* 162

NESAM. *See* Nucleus of Mozambican Students (NESAM)

New Left *1:* 14

"New Song," *1:* 20

New Rhenish Gazette 2: 374

New York Communist 3: 455

Newer Ideas of Peace 1: 7

Newcomb Cleveland Prize *1:* 114

Newton, Huey *1:* 72 (ill.), 73,76

NFWA. *See* National Farm Workers Association (NFWA)